# JAMES CAMERON

*For Alastair, Alex, Andy E, Andy T and Ian – aka The Mob, aka Rough Justice, aka The Friday Elves – with whom I lived and breathed James Cameron's early movies.*

First published in Great Britain in 2025 by Greenfinch
An imprint of Quercus
Part of John Murray Group

ISBN 978-1-52944-459-9
EBOOK ISBN 978-1-52944-460-5

10 9 8 7 6 5 4 3 2 1

Cover design by Luke Bird
Interior design by Ginny Zeal
Printed and bound in Dubai by Oriental Press

MIX
Paper | Supporting
responsible forestry
FSC® C004800

Papers used by Quercus are from well-managed forests and other responsible sources.

Quercus
Carmelite House
50 Victoria Embankment
London EC4Y 0DZ

John Murray Group
Part of Hodder & Stoughton Limited
An Hachette UK company

The authorised representative in the EEA is Hachette Ireland,
8 Castlecourt Centre, Dublin 15, D15 XTP3, Ireland (email: info@hbgi.ie)

ICONIC DIRECTORS SERIES

# JAMES CAMERON

## THE COMPLETE UNOFFICIAL GUIDE

DAN JOLIN

greenfinch

# CONTENTS

*'Sometimes we are lucky enough to know
that our lives have been changed, to discard the
old, embrace the new, and run headlong
down an immutable course.'*

JACQUES COUSTEAU, OCEANOGRAPHER

**ABOVE:** Sam Worthington and Zoë Saldaña as Jake Sully and Neytiri in James Cameron's revolutionary sci-fi adventure *Avatar*.

# INTRODUCTION

'Larger than life' is an overused phrase in the entertainment business, where superlatives are part of everyday speech. Even so, it is hard to think of a living filmmaker whom it better describes than James Cameron.

Let's start at the bottom line. In late 1997 and 1998 Cameron broke box-office records when *Titanic* – a film that only months earlier was predicted to be a turkey – took more than $1.8 billion worldwide (with re-releases since adding another half billion). That record remained unbroken until he released *Avatar* 12 years later, which, to date, has grossed $2.9 billion. Because evidently only James Cameron could beat James Cameron at the box office. And while his next *Avatar* instalment *The Way of Water* did not make quite as much, it is still the third-biggest movie ever, with a worldwide haul of $2.3 billion.

None of these were director-for-hire jobs. Cameron also wrote, produced and edited the movies (as well as creating vivid concept artworks). This makes him an auteur operating at the highest level of the blockbuster. If any single director has cracked the code of global cinematic reach, it is Cameron. Not bad for a guy who started out throwing rubber piranhas at actors.

Cameron spends big, too. His *Terminator* sequel *Judgment Day* was, in 1991, the most expensive movie ever made. . .until he made *True Lies* in 1994, which was the first production to exceed $100 million – a budget he doubled with *Titanic* three years later, and has more than tripled with his *Avatar* sequels. But, even though he takes big risks with mountains of Hollywood studio cash, Cameron is not some profligate maverick. He has funded genuine innovations, such as the underwater filmmaking technology he developed for *The Abyss*, the deep-sea filming equipment required for *Titanic*'s modern-day segments (which

visited the real wreck at the bottom of the Atlantic), and the vast leaps forward in performance capture he oversaw during the productions of his *Avatar* films.

Beyond the bean counting, Cameron's movies tackle big themes. Nuclear war, artificial intelligence, environmental devastation. . .He likes to push our species to the very precipice of survival. And then give us faith in the power of individuals – often women – to pull us back from it. Our fraught relationship with technology courses through his scripts, whether it manifests as

**ABOVE:** Cameron in his element, on the vast Mexican water-tank set of *Titanic*, with his young stars Leonardo DiCaprio and Kate Winslet.

killer cyborgs or supposedly unsinkable Edwardian cruise liners. 'I see our potential destruction and our potential salvation as human beings coming from technology and how we use it,' he said in 2003. 'How we master it and how we prevent it from mastering us.' Cameron himself, of course, being a proven master.

As a film industry personality, he looms no less large. For the first half of his career, he was considered by many to be the scariest man in Hollywood; a tyrannical perfectionist with a militaristic mindset, notorious for his cutting remarks and on-set tantrums. To his friends, including megastar Arnold Schwarzenegger, this was a whole other side to his personality, earning Cameron the nickname 'Mij' ('Jim' backwards). 'When I get to the end of a film, 50 per cent of my crew usually believes I'm a complete asshole,' Cameron said in 1994. 'The other 50 per cent *knows* I'm a complete asshole.' Yet most of those who criticize his high-pressure managerial style also recognize that 'Mij' works harder than anybody else on his sets, never hesitating to muck in when required. During the *Titanic* shoot, for example, Cameron grabbed an axe and happily joined his crew in hacking away at the mammoth blocks of ice that arrived on set for the film's post-iceberg-collision scenes.

Away from Hollywood, he is famously no less industrious or risk averse. Cameron's greatest love is for the ocean, exploring its inkiest depths while engineering new ways to reach them. There is no obstacle, it seems, that he cannot overcome to see what's on the other side. 'I'm an explorer at heart, a filmmaker by trade,' he once said. 'There is nothing that Hollywood can offer more tantalizing or powerful than the chance to explore a place nobody has ever seen.' Even though he is the guy who made cinema bigger than it has ever been before, cinema itself just is not big enough for James Cameron, it seems.

I was first pulled into the orbit of Planet Cameron before I was old enough to see his films on the big screen. During the 1980s, I experienced *The Terminator* and *Aliens* on VHS. Repeatedly. With my teenage friends I watched and rewatched these lean, mean sci-fi thrillers until they became part of our adolescent lexicon, their gung-ho dialogue still to this day ingrained in my memory. This was, if you will forgive my testosteronic phrasing, science fiction with *balls*. Even though, quite brilliantly, its heroes were women. And it was in drawing the connections between these two early films – from their

**ABOVE:** Cameron (right) with his friend and leading man Arnold Schwarzenegger, on the set of *Terminator 2: Judgment Day*.

dark, gritty, hardware-toting style, to the cool, shared cast members (Michael Biehn, Bill Paxton, Lance Henriksen) – that I first became cognisant of the role of movie director, and understood it as a creative force. I knew that here was someone whose every work I needed to seek out.

Not that he was prolific. Being a James Cameron fan requires patience. But that just makes each of his films more of an event. Over the years, they have heavily underlined the sheer sensory impact of cinema and, honestly, hit me with some of the most impressive big-screen moments I have ever experienced. The strange, watery tentacle of *The Abyss*, impossibly writhing its way through a seafloor oil rig. The T-1000 remoulding itself to pass through a set of iron bars in *Terminator 2*. . .And then getting its pistol caught for a moment as it steps forward (such a great little touch; even killer liquid-metal robots slip up). The engrossingly chilling moment in *Titanic* when Rose, axe in hand, takes a fearful beat amid the sinking hulk; the lights go out, and all we hear are the booming, creaking death groans of the ship accompanied by her desperate gasps. The first swim of the Na'vi in *Avatar: The Way of Water*, which, in high-def 3D IMAX transformed the Odeon Leicester Square into an extra-terrestrial aquarium. In short, James Cameron has punctuated my movie-viewing life with some of its biggest 'wows'.

He may not garner the same cineastic respect as other filmmakers, and he certainly has his weak points and blind spots. But Cameron's tangible contribution to the form cannot be denied. As I hope to express in the following pages, he strives (often mercilessly so) to entertain in the broadest sense possible, pushing the cinematic experience to new heights, while attempting to share with us his justifiable concerns about the world and our tenuous place in it.

He is a box-office alchemist, a visual-effects conjurer and a bona-fide pioneer. The 'larger-than-life' guy who, on screen, whatever the cost, has made life seem larger for the rest of us.

**RIGHT:** Cameron on the set of *Avatar*, doing what he does best: building new sci-fi worlds.

*'Pure technolust'*

# GENESIS AND XENOGENESIS
# 1954–78

**D**uring an on-stage interview at the British Film Institute in April 2003, James Cameron was asked by an audience member what advice he would give an aspiring filmmaker. 'I have a smart-ass answer,' he replied, 'which is, if you have to ask that question, you're not gonna make it.' However, he then conceded this was not fair. 'The point is that everybody's going to have to find their own path.'

Cameron's own path was long and winding, beginning 2,250 kilometres away from Hollywood, in Chippawa, Canada, near Niagara Falls. He had moved there from the small town of Kapuskasing in 1966 at the age of 12, with his parents Philip (an electrical engineer) and Shirley (an artist turned full-time parent) and his four younger siblings. By this time, Cameron had already revealed himself as a resourceful, risk-taking kid, with a taste for invention and adventure. When he was not overachieving at school, 'He was always into blowing things up,' recalled family friend Susan Gaede. 'He always seemed to be doing dangerous things.'

Young Jim marshalled the help of his brother Mike to build model rockets, though they also created a hot-air balloon from stitched-together dry-cleaning bags (reported in the local news as a UFO), and even a full-scale, rock-flinging trebuchet. At one time, foreshadowing his future nautical adventures, Cameron constructed a mini-submersible from a mayonnaise jar, an erector set and a bucket, into which he put a mouse before lowering it to the bottom of the Chippawa Creek. ('The mouse was fine,' he said years later. 'I would never be cruel to animals.')

He has since wondered if such antics were an attempt to gain the 'respect or interest' of his strict, engineer father. But, like his mother, the teen Cameron was also a keen artist, learning to draw with Marvel Comics like *Spider-Man* and *X-Men*, and he initially

**RIGHT:** Cameron taught himself to draw using Marvel comics like *The Amazing Spider-Man*.

fantasized about becoming a comic-book artist himself. 'If you look at a comic book, frame for frame, they're cut like films: close-up, wide shot, etc.,' he said in 1986. 'Doing comics, you learn how to create a visual narrative.' However, his inspirations extended far beyond the bam-pow of superheroes. Shirley would often drive him to the Royal Ontario Museum 130 kilometres away, where he would spend hours sketching the exhibits. Drawing, he said, was his way of 'owning' things.

Around this time, Cameron also became 'a rabid consumer of sci-fi'. He 'gorged' himself on pulp paperbacks and magazines and stayed up late on Friday nights watching *Creature Features* on TV, developing 'an encyclopedic knowledge of every alien invasion strategy [and] every monster-creation method.' Over the years his imagination expanded, filling with visions of epic cosmic adventures that TV and cinema had yet to match.

Then, when he was 15, he saw Stanley Kubrick's seminal, genre-redefining *2001: A Space Odyssey* (1968). For the first time, something on a screen came close to matching his imagination. 'I learned so much about what the power of a movie could be from that,' he said years later. 'The film made me dizzy. . .I was fascinated by the effects, because I had no idea how they were done. I just couldn't believe my eyes. It was dazzling.' In this moment, Cameron's enthusiasms for art, science-fiction and engineering fused and focused into a single realization: he wanted to make movies. The only problem was, 'Film directors come from Hollywood, not from Niagara Falls.'

In early 1971, Philip Cameron had some big family news. His employer had offered him a promotion in a new location, far away in Los Angeles, California. It would be a big move to a new country, so he and Shirley sat down with each of his kids individually, to answer their questions and hear their concerns. Philip and Shirley's talk with their eldest was a quick one. 'Los Angeles? Isn't that near Hollywood?' the 16-year-old asked, excitedly. 'Can we leave tomorrow?'

By this time, the *2001*-inspired Cameron had already started experimenting with his dad's Super 8 camera. He made 'little films' such as the Kubrick-referencing *Niagara, or How I Learned to Stop Worrying and Love the Falls*, though they gradually became more ambitious, involving spaceship-model building and even snatching a thundering close-up of a passing train by lying dangerously close to the tracks. But he sensed he would never get anywhere living in Chippawa, so the prospect of moving to the heart of the North American film industry could not have been more promising.

However, the job was actually located in the suburb of Brea, Orange County, 53 kilometres southeast of Los Angeles. So near and yet so far from the Dream Factory. It was so not what Cameron had hoped, he even gave up on his dream for a while, focusing instead on studying physics at Fullerton, a junior college, before switching to English literature. 'I didn't know if I wanted to be a scientist or an artist,' he later reflected. In the end, he gave up on both, dropping out 'to experience the world a little bit,' even though, aside from an epic, hitchhiking trip back to Niagara Falls, 'I didn't really end up experiencing the world. I experienced Brea, California.'

Thus began Cameron's 'blue-collar' life, working as machinist, a high-school janitor, a gas-station attendant and a truck driver for the Brea Unified School District. During this time, he fell in love with Sharon Williams, who worked as a waitress and would eventually become his first wife. He also formed two important friendships, with fellow movie-maker wannabes William Wisher Jr and Randall Frakes. 'What created a lifelong bond between us was our mutual passion for sci-fi,' wrote Frakes of Cameron. With his and Wisher's encouragement, Cameron started writing, carrying a clipboard and yellow notepaper wherever he went, scrawling down ideas late into the night. 'The first thing I ever read by Jim was the first five chapters of his *Necropolis*, a post-apocalyptic novel he had handwritten on a legal pad in pencil,' recalled Frakes. 'His instinctive skill as a prose writer was evident, his dynamic ideas leaping off the page with dramatic intensity.'

**ABOVE:** Engineer and inventor Mike Cameron, James' younger brother, in 2005 documentary *Aliens of the Deep*.

Then came the next movie to shake Cameron's world: *Star Wars*, released when he was 22 years old, in May 1977. If *2001* inspired him to make movies by trying to figure out how it was done, *Star Wars* infuriated him by getting there first. 'I was really upset when I saw *Star Wars*,' he said. 'That was the movie that *I* wanted to make. After seeing that movie I got very determined. I decided to get busy.'

Attending film school had not been an option for Cameron. Neither he nor his parents could afford it. In retrospect, he decided it was for the best. 'Film school really screws you up,' he said in 1991. 'I think the basic requirement of directing is being able to anticipate what an audience wants to see.'

Not that he specifically wanted to become a director. 'When I got started in film,' he said in 1986, 'it was pure technolust. I just wanted to learn how all that stuff was done on a technical level as opposed to an aesthetic level.' He started spending his weekends in the library of the University of Southern California, absorbing and Xeroxing texts on such techniques as front projection (which finally answered some of his questions about *2001*) and optical printing.

But theory was not enough. Cameron was, and still is, a very hands-on kind of guy. He began purchasing lenses and filmmaking equipment, even at one point laying a dolly track on the floor of his and Sharon's small apartment, much to her understandable concern and annoyance. He also brought his dad's old Super 8 out of retirement and resumed making short films, trying once more to bring even a sliver of his mind's-eye images to the screen, with whatever limited resources he could muster.

Such endeavours reached their peak in 1978, when a friend of Wisher's revealed that his father was the accountant for a group of Orange County dentists seeking to invest in film production as a tax shelter. Seizing the opportunity, Cameron, Wisher and Frakes put together a presentation of 10 or so ideas, all 'pretty commercial

**ABOVE:** With its astonishing visual effects, George Lucas' 1977 mega-hit *Star Wars* spurred Cameron to make his own laser-blasting features.

exploitational-type things,' Cameron said, including a full-on space opera he and Frakes had concocted, titled *Xenogenesis*. It concerned a 'last-ditch mission to save humanity from a giant black hole,' as Cameron summarized. This involved sending a spaceship full of human embryos to find a new planet, via a journey that would take in a love-triangle romance and battles with giant robots, leading to a climax that saw the rise of a new, blue-skinned species of extra-terrestrial human.

Clearly with the success of *Star Wars* in mind, the dentists chose this idea, giving Cameron and co $20,000 in cash to start up. Obviously it was not nearly enough, but, as Cameron put it, 'I was game. I had nothing to lose.' Well, except for his job, which he promptly quit, refusing even to work out his two weeks' notice so he could start on *Xenogenesis* as soon as possible.

Renting space in an Orange County industrial park, and making use of Fullerton College's eye clinic as a location, Cameron immediately assumed the role of director. He also took on the visual effects, designing and building all the required models from scratch, including a laser-blasting sentry droid that would later reappear as the gigantic Hunter-Killer in *The Terminator*'s Future War scenes. 'Everybody did a little bit of everything on that film,' recalled Wisher of a frenetic production that roped in all their friends and families (while he himself starred). 'But Jim was definitely the engine pushing it.'

It was a steep learning curve. 'We were totally rank amateurs,' said Cameron. The first few days of the shoot were spent learning how to load the 35mm cameras and change the lenses. But the experience enabled him to properly try out all the techniques he had been teaching himself, such as forced perspectives and the use of glass mattes to enhance real backgrounds in-camera, as well as rigging explosions and animating laser beams.

In the end, the dentists lost their nerve and backed out of the project, so *Xenogenesis* was never completed. Cameron was not disheartened. He had 12 minutes of self-made visual-effects-packed footage he could use as a showreel.

**ABOVE:** The Future War sequences in 1984's *The Terminator* harked back to Cameron's 12-minute career proof-of-concept *Xenogenesis*.

Centred on a battle between a pair of huge stop-motion robots (one of which is controlled, not unlike *Aliens'* power loader, by heroine Lori, played by Margaret Umbel), it was proof of his talent and resourcefulness. 'An amazing piece of work for a bunch of dumb shits that didn't know what they were doing,' he said. This would finally be his ticket to Hollywood. Even if it only got him in through one of its smallest side entrances.

# NEW WORLD PICTURES AND PIRANHA II
## 1979–82

**R**oger Corman is one of the most celebrated names in US independent cinema. During the 1960s, while at American International Pictures, he made his name directing Edgar Allan Poe adaptations fronted by Vincent Price, and low-budget counterculture curios such as *The Little Shop of Horrors*, *X: The Man with the X-ray Eyes*, and *The Trip*. Later, as a producer, he broke in upcoming directors, including Francis Ford Coppola, Jonathan Demme and Ron Howard, with trashy fare *Dementia 13*, *Caged Heat* and *Grand Theft Auto*, respectively. In 1970, Corman set up New World Pictures, complete with its own mini studio in an old Venice Beach lumber yard, to turn out exploitation cheapies, often shamelessly ripping off whatever was popular at the time. In the wake of *Jaws* and its first sequel, for example, came New World's *Piranha* (the directorial debut of Joe Dante). And after *Star Wars* there was *Battle Beyond the Stars*.

Written by future indie auteur John Sayles and directed by Jimmy Murakami, this space-based take on *Seven Samurai* and its Western remake *The Magnificent Seven* took Corman's outfit to a new level of production value, requiring a hefty budget of $2 million. When the callow and hungry 25-year-old Cameron knocked on New World's door with his *Xenogenesis*

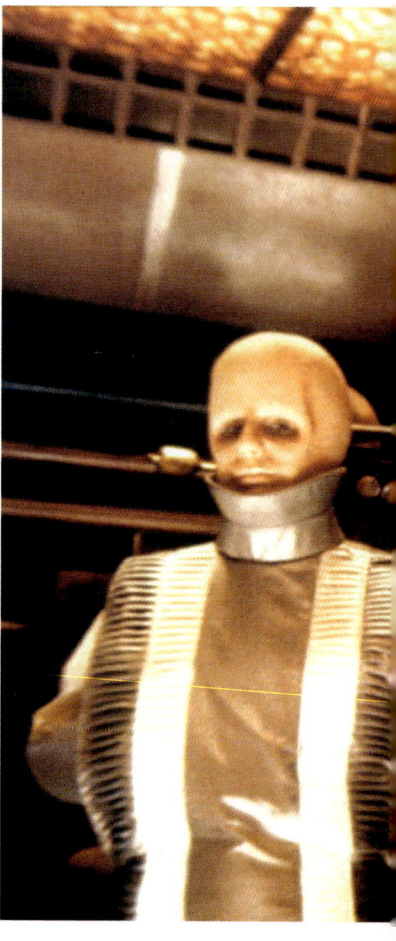

**ABOVE:** Morgan Woodward (centre) as the reptilian Cayman, with his 'Kelvin' sidekicks who communicate via body heat – just a few of the colourful characters in *Battle Beyond the Stars*.

reel tucked under one arm, it was fortuitous timing. He was destined to become Corman's most impressive protégé yet.

'I went through that place like crap through a goose,' said Cameron of New World Pictures. On the strength of *Xenogenesis*, he was hired as a model builder by Chuck Comisky, head of New World's recently formed FX department. It did not take him long to make his mark. When Corman sent his 24-year-old, Stanford-graduate

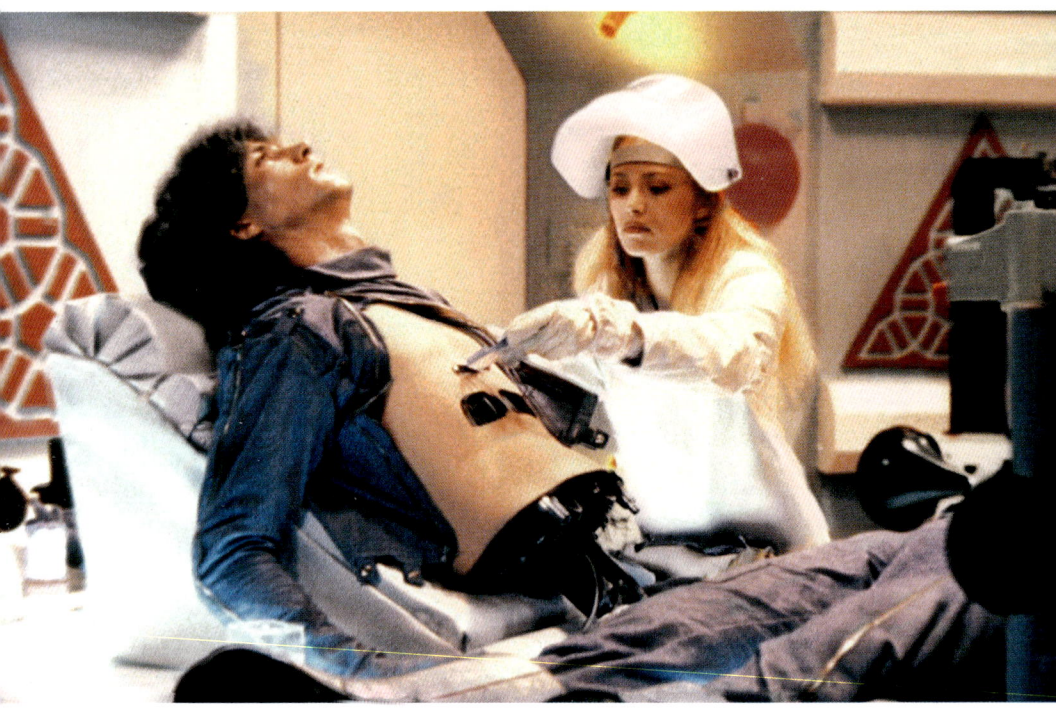
ABOVE: Darlanne Fluegel as the tech-savvy Nanelia, tending
to one of her robots in *Battle Beyond the Stars*.

assistant Gale Anne Hurd down to the lumber yard to report on preproduction, she was greeted by Cameron, who confidently gave her a tour of the model shop. Given his 'very commanding presence', she assumed this tall blond guy was the department head, but he revealed he'd only been there a few days.

Soon after, Corman himself noticed the diligent go-getter. Seeking a striking look for *Battle Beyond the Stars'* lead spaceship Nell (voiced by Lynn Carlin), he held a competition among the design team. Cameron, the story goes, triumphed with a drawing that unsubtly emphasized the craft's feminine personality, not only through its front-view similarity to the female reproductive system (complete with fallopian-tube gun turrets), but also its consciously

## When Cameron met Carpenter:
### *Escape From New York* (1981)

John Carpenter was a filmmaker that Cameron admired. With 1978's *Halloween*, he had created a tight, low-budget horror hit that elevated a B-movie genre and established himself as an impressive new talent. In 1981, while at New World Pictures, Cameron pounced on the chance to collaborate with Carpenter on his dystopian prison-break adventure *Escape From New York*.

Cameron learned from the film's production designer Joe Alves that Carpenter was frustrated by the prohibitively expensive quotes he was being given by visual-effects companies. So, he stepped forward and offered New World's considerably cheaper services, highlighting the front-projection process he had engineered for *Battle Beyond the Stars*, and ultimately earning himself a credit on *Escape From New York* as 'director of photography: special visual effects/matte artwork'.

One of Cameron's finest problem-solving moments was devising a convincing 3D map of New York that appeared on a control-panel screen. He achieved this by constructing scale cardboard models of Manhattan's buildings, painting them black, outlining them with DayGlo paint, and weaving a camera between them.

While it was hardly a shoulder-to-shoulder collaboration with Carpenter, the director did recall being impressed by this plucky and inventive crew member. 'Jim Cameron's work just knocked me on my ass,' he said.

smooth and voluptuous curves. 'You can see it has a hip-pelvic configuration,' said Cameron, who was inspired by the bio-mechanical creations of Swiss artist H R Giger. 'Then at the back you have the mons pubis, and the thrusters are designed to look like thighs.' Corman was delighted by the 'spaceship with tits', though the other members of the model shop, disgruntled at being upstaged by this brash newcomer, mocked it.

Not that Cameron was bothered. Within weeks, he had secured a promotion to the newly created role of Head of Process Projection.

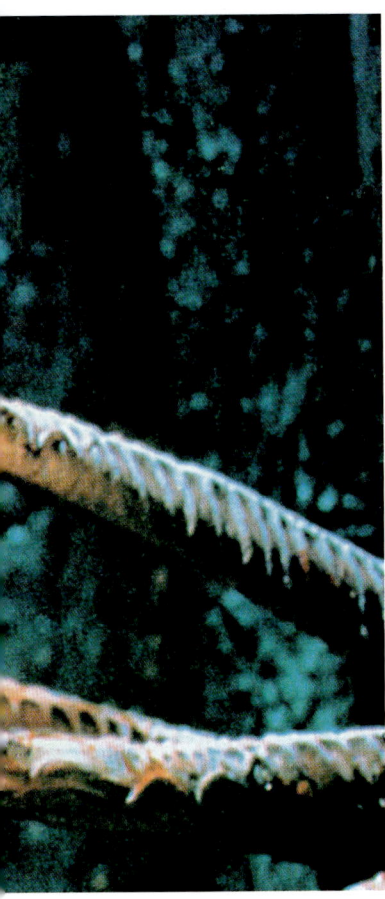

This happened after he convinced Corman that the film would benefit from the same front-projection technique Kubrick had pioneered on *2001: A Space Odyssey*, in order to blend the film's model-based FX work with the performances of the actors. Not only that, but Cameron bluffed that he had the expertise to rig it up – despite only having studied front projection during his visits to the USC library. Even so, he pulled it off, eliciting further opprobrium from his bewildered co-workers.

Soon after, roughly one month into Cameron's New World incursion, Corman offered him the role of art director (in addition to his other responsibilities), after firing his predecessor for failing to complete the sufficient number of spaceship-interior and planetary-surface set builds. Once more, with supreme self-confidence trumping experience – of which he had none – Cameron accepted. 'And suddenly there I was, this little martinet in charge of a crew of 60 or 70 people.'

Despite twice firing Cameron (who just returned to work the next day), and resenting his reasonable demands for pay hikes (Cameron quadrupled his salary within a few months), Corman was hugely impressed. 'I remember the young James Cameron as a ferociously hard-working perfectionist who never hesitated to give

200 per cent of his ideas, energy and talent to someone else's movie,' he wrote in 1997. Though Cameron's willingness to pull 85-hour shifts and sleep at the studio came with a personal cost. His marriage to Sharon fell apart as he fully turned his attention to his new career – regardless of the quality of its output.

Cameron's next movie at New World was another sci-fi rip-off, this time of Ridley Scott's *Alien*, in the dubious form of 1981's *Galaxy of Terror*, directed by Bruce D Clark. *Battle Beyond the Stars* was a largely harmless and daffy family-friendly romp, marred only by one strong suggestion of off-screen sexual violence, when two bored, leering mutant baddies decide to kidnap a young bride. But *Galaxy of Terror* pushes its interstellar horror with a thoroughly repellent inter-species rape-murder scene, as actress Taaffe O'Connell is stripped naked, covered in slime and attacked by an alien maggot-monster... which was designed by Cameron, whose job title by now was production designer.

This was, he later admitted, 'one of the darkest moments in my film career.' Corman 'always had some form of sexual attack in his movies,' he said. 'For him, it always came down to what sold best at the drive-in movies in the South or whatever.' But despite his distaste, Cameron threw himself into this grubby, forgettable project with as much enthusiasm as he could muster, alongside visual-effects-artist siblings Robert and Dennis Skotak, with whom he would later collaborate on *Aliens*. 'I felt like I could at least impose some good ideas on the project through my designs,' he said.

While working on *Galaxy of Terror*, Cameron observed Clark directing the actors and setting up shots. For the first time, he thought about becoming a director himself. 'I had wanted to make films, and I'd understood at some intellectual level that the director was the person who was most in charge creatively, but I had never pictured myself in that role,' he said. During this

**ABOVE:** *Galaxy of Terror*'s motley ensemble included *Happy Days* star Erin Moran, *Falcon Crest*'s Edward Albert and Zalman King, later best known for directing erotic thrillers.

production he concluded it was a job that he could do better than the directors he had worked with.

Cameron's opportunity came when Corman recommended him to Greco-Italian producer Ovidio G Assonitis, who, via an international distribution deal with New World and Warner Bros, was overseeing the sequel to *Piranha*. Lacking any of the self-knowing wit of Dante's original (which, like *Battle Beyond the Stars*, was scripted by John Sayles), this grimly priapic ultra-cheapie located its fish-assaulted holiday resort in Jamaica, and upgraded (if that is the right word) its ravenous killers to mutated flying-fish hybrids. It was, Cameron later deadpanned, 'The best flying piranha movie ever made.'

It was also the least auspicious directorial debut he, or indeed any filmmaker, could have hoped for.

Cameron knew the script was awful, and that he was letting himself in for a trying time, shooting far from home with a mostly Italian crew. But it was another chance to prove his worth. Besides, 'What you learn working for New World, and on that type of film, is just "Go for it,"' he said. 'There's always a way to get it done and make it presentable.' Unless, that is, you are deliberately set up to fail.

When he arrived in Ocho Rios, Jamaica, having punched up the risible script as best he could and taught himself some Italian, he was dismayed to discover that pre-production had begun without him. Even worse, the rubber flying-piranha puppets the crew had made were 'abominable' and not fit for filming. So, before he started rolling on his first feature as director, Cameron was back to desperate grunt work, redesigning and repainting all the prop fish himself. Within weeks, he would be literally throwing them from off-camera at bikini-clad *Penthouse* models to simulate a killer-fish attack. Just another day at the *Piranha II* office.

The production was so low budget, there was no wardrobe department. To convincingly dress his star Lance Henriksen as resort cop Steve, Cameron talked a Henriksen-sized waiter into selling him his uniform and adapted it himself. He had to find his own locations, too. For a mortuary break-in scene, in which the film's heroine, Anne (Tricia O'Neil) and her creepy stalker boyfriend (Steve Marachuk) try to gather evidence of this flappy new species, Cameron managed to secure a real morgue. Unfortunately, when he arrived to shoot there, he found it had real bodies in it. After he set up a divider to hide them, some staff came in during the lunch break to remove one of the corpses. But when a mishap led to the body spilling its guts over the set floor, Cameron had to hastily mop up the viscera before his cast and crew returned.

**ABOVE:** *Piranha II*'s Anne (Tricia O'Neil, centre), can be regarded as a prototype for the resourceful heroines of James Cameron's later films.

Even more worryingly, the budget could not cover stunt people. In the scene where Steve jumps into the sea from a police helicopter, Henriksen had to take the 12-metre plunge himself, and broke his right hand. The accident could not be laid at Cameron's door, however, because by this point, Assonitis had fired him. What Cameron had not known going into *Piranha II* was that Assonitis had no intention of letting him 'go for it'. In order to secure his deal with Warner Bros, the producer needed an American director's name on the film, but he always intended to direct it himself. 'The whole time I was like a sacrificial lamb,' said Cameron. A few weeks into the shoot, he was taken aside by one of Assonitis assistants and laid off. His footage, he was told,

was awful. Having been denied permission to see any of it, he did not know if there was any truth to this, which vexed him more than the actual firing.

So much so, that, after returning to the United States and stewing for the next few weeks, Cameron flew to Rome, where the film was being edited, to have it out with Assonitis, who had also refused to take his name off the film ('I had no legal power to influence him from Pomona, California,' said Cameron. 'I didn't even know an attorney.') Unused to being challenged like this, Assonitis assented to Cameron viewing the footage. The good news: Cameron's work was *not* disastrous. It was, he realized, as well shot as it could have been under the circumstances. 'I thought, "You know what? I can actually do this." I'd just fallen in with a pack of thieves and whackos.' But the bad news was, Assonitis was cutting it together terribly. 'It made me very mistrustful of other people who have creative power on a film,' he said. 'Very mistrustful.'

After raging at the producer the next day, Cameron decided that if his name was going to be on the movie, he was going to turn it into something watchable. While staying at a nearby backstreet pensione, living on room-service leftovers he found in the corridors and suffering from flu, he sneaked into the editing room and spent long, hot nights secretly re-cutting the footage into a more acceptable shape, with a little more coherence and a lot less gratuitous nudity.

Sadly, we will never know what this unsanctioned Director's Cut of *Piranha II* looked like, as Cameron was eventually discovered, threatened with legal action, and urged to return to the United States. But while he has understandably disowned the movie that

**LEFT:** *Piranha II* was shot on real Jamaican beaches, where the make-up department splashed around a lot of fake blood.

still bears his first credit as director, it does exhibit some of his fingerprints, even circumstantially. There is the presence of Henriksen, of course, with whom Cameron bonded, and who would return for *The Terminator* and *Aliens*. O'Neil, meanwhile, plays a tough, resourceful woman who drives the plot, like *The Terminator*'s

Sarah Connor and *Aliens'* Ripley – and she would also act again for Cameron, many years later, in *Titanic*. Speaking of which, *Piranha II* has a prevalence of underwater footage, with diving scenes (the aquatically inclined Cameron was, by this time, a qualified scuba diver) and a shipwreck – the source of all those genetically engineered little monsters.

None of which made the experience any less disastrous for its nominal director. After his Roman misadventure, the young filmmaker was alienated and penniless. What was supposed to be his big break had come close to breaking *him*. But he was too bloody-minded to let an unscrupulous producer and a bunch of flying fish scupper his nascent career. 'When I got back from *Piranha II*,' he said, 'I knew that I was never going to get offered another movie unless I came up with something myself. I had to write a film.'

Fortunately, he had recently had an idea. Or rather, a vision. One day in his scuzzy pensione, half-starved, isolated and shivering with fever, he suffered a horrifyingly vivid nightmare: of 'a metal skeleton coming out of fire' and crawling along the floor towards him with a knife in one metallic hand. As if it only had one single purpose: to terminate him.

*'There's a storm coming in'*

# THE
# TERMINATOR
## 1984

The end of the world had been on James Cameron's mind for much of his life. He was eight years old when the United States and the Soviet Union came to the brink of mutually assured destruction over the Cuban Missile Crisis; a disturbing reality that was literally brought home by a pamphlet he discovered on a coffee table, which provided instructions for building a civilian fallout shelter. Suddenly, he realized, 'the world as we knew it could end at any moment.' This fear/fascination would be nourished by the countless sci-fi novels, movies and TV shows he absorbed over the following decades, until he himself was in a position to depict a nuclear Armageddon like no-one ever had before.

*Piranha II* aside, every James Cameron movie until *Titanic* features nuclear weapons in some form, whether referred to or witnessed directly. Only one is actively prevented from exploding (in *The Abyss*). Most detonate – even in Cameron's only comedy, *True Lies*. In *Aliens*, he goes as far as presenting atomic annihilation as a solution, rather than a problem. 'I say we take off and nuke the site from orbit,' says the ever-decisive heroine Ripley (Sigourney Weaver). 'It's the only way to be sure.' (The ultimate big boom, however, is not a deployed nuke, but an atmosphere-processor meltdown with the equivalent megatonnage.)

*The Terminator* marks the beginning not only of Cameron's directing career proper, but also of a suitably premillennial cycle, very much the product of Cold War-era anxiety – though Cameron did here give it a novel techno-fear spin. Due to budget limitations, *The Terminator*'s apocalypse is unseen, happening sometime between the film's present-day events – in which an unsuspecting LA waitress named Sarah Connor (Linda Hamilton) becomes the target of a cyborg hitman from the future (Arnold Schwarzenegger) – and its

**RIGHT:** Linda Hamilton as Sarah Connor, who Cameron partly based on his first wife Sharon Williams.

depictions of a war-torn Los Angeles in 2029, where human survivors led by Sarah's son John wage a last-ditch guerrilla campaign against the laser-blasting hardware of an artificial intelligence named Skynet. 'There was a nuclear war,' explains Kyle Reese (Michael Biehn), a soldier sent back in time by Sarah's son to protect her. 'It was the machines, Sarah. Defence network computers. New. . .powerful. . .hooked into everything, trusted to run it all. They say it got smart, a new order of intelligence. Then it saw all people as a threat, not just the ones on the other side. Decided our fate in a microsecond: extermination.' It is not the Russians or Americans who torch the planet in Cameron's future-shock tale, but our own clever (too clever) computing tools.

It is a hugely prescient notion, to the degree that the film itself has become a shorthand for modern concerns about artificial intelligence, whether referenced comedically, such as in Mike Judge's tech-bro sitcom *Silicon Valley* ('Okay, but see, the problem is. . .*Terminator*'), or in academic writing by philosophers and roboticists. 'There are more recent, and more plausible, influential films about AI,' wrote author Dorian Lynskey on the film's 40th anniversary, 'but when it comes to the dangers of the technology, *The Terminator* reigns supreme.'

**ABOVE:** *The Terminator*'s Future War scenes, which take place in 2029, were the result of extensive and intensive model work by Fantasy II Film Effects.

Cameron himself loves to highlight this. 'We are no closer to interstellar travel than we were back in [science-fiction pioneer] Hugo Gernsback's day,' he said in 2018. 'But we are a hell of a lot closer to *Terminator*.' He has attended symposiums of AI scientists where, he laughs, they roll their eyes and call him 'that Skynet guy'. But, he continues to insist, 'the point is that no technology has ever not been weaponized. And do we really want to be fighting something smarter than us that isn't us on our own world? I don't think so. It could literally be the end of the world.' As it was in Sarah Connor's not-too-distant future.

But the 28-year-old James Cameron did not set out to make an enduring commentary on AI when he started writing *The Terminator* in 1982, in his one-bedroom apartment in Tarzana, California. He did aim for it to have 'some sort of sociopolitical significance between the lines,' he said, like the sci-fi he loved. But nothing so specific. Fuelled by his chrome-skulled fever dream and a vital need to rinse the career-tainting aftertaste of *Piranha II*, Cameron's primary ambition was a little less high-falutin': to create, as he put it, 'some sort of really definitive robot story.'

To help achieve this, Cameron partnered up with his former New World colleague Gale Anne Hurd, who since also leaving Corman's employ had set up her own production company, Pacific Western Productions. The pair had clicked and stayed in touch since that first encounter during the early days of *Battle Beyond the Stars*, and Hurd was impressed by Cameron's first treatment for *The Terminator*. Especially as, for all its sci-fi trappings, he had calibrated it to be achievable on a small budget.

'I kind of backed into it because it was like, "All right, what kind of film will they let me direct?"' Cameron said. '"It's got to be something I could shoot on the streets of present-day LA, where I live."' Yet it would also have to feature his killer robot, and enable him to exercise his special-effects skills. 'Well, there's only two ways to get something extraordinary here,' he reasoned. 'Either from space or from somewhere else in time. . .' He settled on time travel, and encased his robot in cheap-to-depict human flesh. The story, he said, 'just kind of dominoed from the parameters of my life and what I needed to do.'

**RIGHT:** Arnold Schwarzenegger as the Terminator – a role that both restyled the movie and redefined his career.

CHAPTER THREE

This sense of necessity extended to the remarkable deal he made with Hurd. In return for the promise that she would not sell the script to any studio that would not accept him as director, he sold her the rights to *The Terminator* for a mere $1. While in the long term this would prove financially costly for Cameron, the gambit worked. Hurd (who soon became the filmmaker's romantic partner, too, and his second wife) kept her word, and Cameron was allowed to direct when the movie was finally picked up by John Daly at Hemdale Film Corporation, which had a distribution arrangement with Orion Pictures, with HBO grabbing the TV rights.

Infamously, to help seal the deal, Cameron sent his *Piranha II* buddy Lance Henriksen into Daly's office in the guise of a Terminator, complete with a torn T-shirt, prosthetic wounds and some cigarette-packet foil over his teeth. After kicking open the door, Henriksen silently settled down opposite Daly, and stared at him, unblinking. Just as the unnerved producer was 'ready to jump out the window,' as the actor recalled, Cameron bustled in with his detailed treatment and artworks, and swiftly blew Daly away with the sheer coherence of his vision. He was granted a budget of $4 million, which, over time, rose to around $6.4 million.

Of course, the executives had some notes. HBO did suggest that Cameron give the central romance between Connor and Reese some more weight and focus, which he happily took on board. 'All my movies are love stories. Just different types of love stories,' he reflected in 2024. However, another exec, whom Cameron has said should 'go unmentioned', requested that Reese have a robot dog. Suffice to say, he did *not* take that on board.

While the director was allowed to make his own call for the role of Sarah – which after considering Jennifer Jason Leigh and Rosanna Arquette, he gave to Hamilton, feeling she had just the right blend of vulnerability and inner strength to pass as 'the mother of the future' – his producers did have thoughts about

**ABOVE:** Hamilton with Michael Biehn as time-travelling soldier Kyle Reese – the first of three roles he'd play for Cameron over the years.

whom he should cast as The Terminator and Reese. For the titular killing machine, they somewhat ironically with hindsight suggested American football star O J Simpson. But Cameron intended to make his Terminator someone leaner and more likely to blend into a crowd — like Henriksen, or perhaps Jürgen Prochnow, who Cameron had loved in German submarine epic

**ABOVE:** The Terminator's gleaming endoskeleton was brought to grim-reaping life by FX wizard Stan Winston.

*Das Boot*. For Reese, meanwhile, they pushed Austrian bodybuilding sensation Arnold Schwarzenegger, who was on a mission to break into the movie big-time and had recently bared his voluminous pecs in John Milius' full-blooded pulp-fantasy adaptation *Conan the Barbarian*.

Cameron knew Schwarzenegger was not right for the role of the tragic, time-travelling soldier. Firstly, he needed an actor capable of portraying both trauma and tenderness as Reese's love for Sarah surfaces ('I came across time for you. . .') – something he found in relative newcomer Biehn, after briefly considering The Police front man Sting. Secondly, Reese has to deliver all the exposition (mostly *during* the chase sequences, the film's so propulsive). Cameron could not imagine audiences swallowing this with Schwarzenegger's thick Austrian accent poured all over it. So, he planned, as he put it, to 'pick a fight with Conan' at their meeting, and use that as an excuse to turn him down.

But, as has now become enshrined in Hollywood lore, things did not go as planned. The big Austrian and the brash Canadian instantly liked each other, with the former impressing the latter both with his positive commentary on the script – focusing, Cameron noticed, more on how the Terminator should be portrayed than Reese – and for picking up the tab when it transpired that Cameron had forgotten his wallet. As they talked, the director recalled, 'I just watched him: the strength of his face impressed me more than his physique.' By the time the meal was over, Cameron was convinced he should ditch his lean, low-key infiltrator concept for the cyborg assassin, and offer the role to Schwarzenegger: 'I pictured him as a human Panzer tank and I knew that it would work.' As soon as he got home, Cameron grabbed his airbrush and rendered a portrait of Schwarzenegger with half his face missing and a red-eyed metal skull revealed beneath. He sent it over to the actor, who was impressed. 'I looked at this painting and I said, "I *am* the Terminator,"' recalled Schwarzenegger. 'So I called Lou [Pitt], my agent, right away, and the deal was made.' (Henriksen was happy to receive the consolation prize of quippy cop Vuckovich, one of the cyborg's 27 victims.)

This switch gave the film a whole new texture. 'It took on a slightly more hyperbolic visual style,' said Cameron. 'It still played realistically, but it became more nightmarish.' Cameron and director of photography Adam Greenberg accentuated Schwarzenegger's presence by shooting him at low angles. 'He loomed over the film,' said Hurd of the actor, who invested the relentless automaton with an unblinking predatory mien that he modelled on a shark, and worked closely with Cameron on ensuring its movements were smooth and methodical, rather than robotically twitchy.

Rumours abounded that the Terminator's dialogue was minimized as a result of Schwarzenegger's casting, down to its sparse but effective 74 words. But Cameron denies this: 'The script didn't change at all,' he confirmed. Three of those words had an impact far beyond anything he or Schwarzenegger could have expected. Just before the film's central set piece, in which the leather-and-sunglasses-decked Terminator storms through a police precinct all guns blazing, his initial enquiry about Connor is rebuffed by a bespectacled desk sergeant (Bruce Kerner, who was also executive in charge of production). 'I'll be back,' Schwarzenegger replies.

'Nobody was more shocked than myself when people laughed at that line,' said Cameron. 'When I wrote it, I didn't even think it would play that well. I just thought it was throwaway.' But the audience engaged with Schwarzenegger in a way that he did not foresee: they were almost rooting for him, in an odd, vicarious way. They instinctively knew what 'I'll be back' meant when *he* said it: that this guy, who takes no crap and can be as rude as he likes, would kick ass. And, sure enough, moments later he smashes a car into the lobby and crushes that dismissive desk sergeant before embarking on a spree that many interpreted as anti-authoritarian. 'Deep down inside all of us there lurks a person who would love to be like him, even if just for two minutes,' Cameron ruminated. 'Everyone would like to walk into the boss' office without using the doorknob.'

Making Schwarzenegger the Terminator was the smartest casting decision Cameron would ever make, at least until he

**ABOVE:** *Piranha II*'s Lance Henriksen as Detective Hal Vukovich, with Paul Winfield as his partner Ed Traxler.

convinced Leonardo DiCaprio to board the *Titanic*. And taking the role was the smartest decision Schwarzenegger ever made. 'Thanks to the film, he became a fully-fledged movie star,' said Hurd. Despite his relatively low screen time, she pointed out, 'his performance is so dominant.' And, of course, that 'throwaway' line became the actor's catchphrase, uttered in the majority of his movies throughout his career.

While Cameron and Schwarzenegger together crafted the Terminator's impressive exterior, the job of bringing its gleaming endoskeleton to life fell primarily to make-up effects designer Stan Winston, who had won two Emmys for his TV work, and had previously created robots for on 1981 sci-fi romcom *Heartbeeps*. As with Schwarzenegger, it was another tight-knit Cameron collaboration, born of mutual respect for a rigorous work ethic. To Cameron, going down the 'guy in a suit' route George Lucas had taken with the droids in *Star Wars* was not an option for something so inherently skeletal, so Winston was required to build a highly detailed, full-size puppet torso. He knew he was taking a lot on, to be achieved for not much money in a very limited amount of time. On top of that, he'd also have to build all the necessary prosthetics for the scenes where the Terminator performs repairs/surgery on itself. But he was impressed enough by Cameron's drawings, and the meticulousness of his brief, to sign up. 'Usually I do my own design work,' he said, 'but in this case there was already a concept that was really quite brilliant and I didn't want to change it. Jim's idea was for the robot to appear as organic as possible.'

Winston's endoskeleton takes over from Schwarzenegger for the climactic confrontation, which unsubtly takes place in an automated factory after the Terminator's fleshy bits are immolated in a spectacular fuel-truck explosion (astonishingly achieved using model work overseen by Joe Viskocil). Presented in parallel with a 60cm-tall, stop-motion version for its full-body scenes (created by VFX outfit Fantasy II), it is a remarkable animatronic creation wrought from urethane, fibreglass and steel, and expertly controlled by a crack team of puppeteers, who somehow imbue it with no less presence than Schwarzenegger. Cameron could not have been happier. 'The Terminator looks like Death,' he said. Sarah Connor 'faces the image of Death or Fate, and survives.'

**RIGHT:** Stan Winston's make-up effects included the impressive 'surgery' scene where the Terminator tends to its own injuries.

Not that Cameron's bosses appreciated this. When required to screen a rough cut for them before the endoskeleton scenes were complete, he made the rookie error of presenting the film with 'scene missing' cards, rather than inserting storyboards or illustrations. Daly and Orion boss Mike Medavoy were so dismayed, they demanded that Cameron end the movie with the truck explosion. The director was furious. 'Guess what? Fuck you! I'm going to finish the film and I'm gonna show you what it's going to look like,' he recalls telling them.

And finish it he did, though because the budget was by now all spent, he completed his final few scenes guerilla-style, without shooting permits. 'We went out and stole shots at the end,' Cameron said, such as the moment where the Terminator has to punch through a car window. 'Quickly, quickly, before the police come!' Schwarzenegger remembers the director telling him. They avoided the cops that morning, but weren't so lucky later. Cameron remembered the day they shot the final scene, of Sarah having her Polaroid taken (the photo that will eventually be given by her son to Reese), by a roadside in the Californian desert. 'There's nothing visible for 20 miles in any direction,' he said, 'and this little glint on the horizon

ABOVE: In wide shots, the full-body Terminator endoskeleton was realized via stop-motion animation, by Fantasy II.

pulls up and it's a cop. I'm like, "You've got to be fucking kidding me."' The policeman demanded to see a filming permit, which Cameron did not have. So, despite being 29 years old, he pretended to be a clueless film student. 'I just bullshitted my way out.'

Even once the film was completed, with Winston and the VFX team's work fully integrated, Orion was mystifyingly unimpressed. 'This is a down-and-dirty exploitation film,' Hurd was told by the studio's head of marketing. 'We're embarrassed to release it. We don't want to screen it for critics, and it'll be out of theatres by the second weekend.' Cameron himself confessed to being a little worried, given the film would be up against David Lynch's sci-fi epic *Dune* and *2001* sequel *2010: The Year We Make Contact*.

As it turned out, *The Terminator* would outperform both those movies, which were notorious flops. Despite Orion effectively dumping the film, it became a word-of-mouth sleeper hit. 'The audience, God bless them, loved the film,' said Hurd. 'They told their friends to go see it. Even with no marketing support, the box office went up by five per cent in the second weekend.' Ultimately, *The Terminator* would make $78.3 million worldwide, buoyed by overwhelmingly positive reviews. *The Hollywood Reporter*, for example, described it as 'a genuine steel metal trap of a movie that may very well be the best picture of its kind since *The Road Warrior* [aka *Mad Max 2*].' Critic Kirk Ellis picked up on its 'pointed comment on our present overmechanization,' and praised Cameron as 'a lean, economical storyteller, setting up his shots for maximum visceral impact.'

The film's success was, Cameron said, 'like a hallucination for me'. He'd so focused on creating it to be viable, he'd almost forgotten to consider that it might also be a success. 'It gave me a lot of courage as a filmmaker, to go on and do other stuff.' These days, the director looks back on the film with fondness but, ever the perfectionist, cannot help highlighting its limitations. 'There are parts of it that are pretty cringeworthy,' he said, 'and parts of it that are like, "Yeah, we did pretty well for the resources that we had available."'

Yet it holds up amazingly well to modern-day scrutiny, with its savvy emphasis on cut-to-the-chase pacing and its slick 'tech-

## Cameron on script: *Rambo: First Blood Part II* (1985)

James Cameron has never been one to sit on his hands. After *The Terminator* was greenlit, the shoot – which was originally supposed to start in Toronto in autumn 1983 – suffered a half-year delay and a serendipitous relocation to LA, thanks to Arnold Schwarzenegger suddenly being forced to make duff fantasy sequel *Conan The Destroyer*. Cameron used this unexpected hiatus, and the buzz he had accrued for his *Terminator* script, to take on a couple of writing gigs. One of these was the sequel to 1982 survival thriller *First Blood*, starring Sylvester Stallone as PTSD-suffering Vietnam vet John Rambo.

Then titled *The Mission*, the concept was that Rambo would be released from prison to return to Vietnam and rescue American prisoners of war still incarcerated there in camps. ('Do we get to win this time?' he asks.) Cameron had, as a younger man, painted a stage backdrop depicting a POW for his local Prisoner of War/Missing in Action program, so it might have come as no surprise that his script spent a lot of time developing the characters of Rambo's rescuees, as well as giving him a wise-ass sidekick with all the best lines.

Stallone, however, was unimpressed. Having accepted the gig on condition that he would be given a final pass of the script, he stripped out anything that diverted too much attention away from the character of Rambo. The sidekick was gone (despite John Travolta at one point being mentioned for the role), and the POWs reduced to bit parts. 'It was almost like they were parachuting into Nam to pick up a six-pack of beer,' sniffed Cameron of the rather less substantial (but no less action-packed) end result. Though he was phlegmatic about this outcome. 'I'm very satisfied with the script I wrote and that's all I can say,' he stated. 'I tend to be very unemotional about my writing when it's done on assignment.' Besides, the other screenplay he had taken on at this time was far more deserving of his attention and effort. That script being *Aliens*.

noir' styling, to use Cameron's own terminology (also the name he gave the nightclub where the Terminator and Reese finally converge on Sarah in glorious slo-mo). While *The Terminator* paved the way for the mindless one-man army actioners of the Reagan era (despite its gun-toting lunk being the *villain*), it also tweaked the brain with its sci-fi sophistication, not least in its adrenalized take on the grandfather paradox (John Connor would never have been born if Skynet had not sent a Terminator back in time to stop him from being born, because then he would not have sent Reese back in time to stop the Terminator and, along the way, father him).

In his review, published on the day of the movie's release in late October 1984, Ellis asked: '*Terminator II*, where are you?' It was a question Cameron would be asked repeatedly, not least by Schwarzenegger, who felt he was 'sitting on a gold mine' and was keen to dig deeper. When the film came out, Cameron was already working on a sequel. Only it was not to *The Terminator*, but someone else's film entirely. And it would be a very different kind of sci-fi-action-horror hybrid.

**ABOVE:** 'Mother of the future' Sarah finally terminates The Terminator during the film's factory-set conclusion.

*'Not bad for a human'*

# ALIENS
## 1986

In the summer of 1983, James Cameron was invited to meet with producers David Giler and Walter Hill (the latter of whom was also a director, whose chase film *The Driver* had influenced *The Terminator*). Four years earlier, they'd had a significant success with British director Ridley Scott's seminal sci-fi horror *Alien*, and having read and loved Cameron's *Terminator* script, wanted to offer him a new sci-fi project they were developing: a cosmic retelling of the *Spartacus* slave-revolt story. 'They wanted the same movie, but with the sword-and-sandal elements intergalactically dressed up,' remembered Cameron. 'A concept I found pretty idiotic.' As he got up to leave, Giler mentioned they had something else he might be interested in: *Alien II*.

The studio behind Scott's original, 20th Century Fox, had been unenthusiastic about a follow-up, citing the diminishing returns of horror sequels, especially one that would require the expensive, world-building production value of a sci-fi movie. But Fox started to warm to the idea when Giler and Hill outlined a concept that they pitched as '*Southern Comfort* meets *The Magnificent Seven*'. As Giler and Hill explained to Cameron, it would be set around 50 years after the crew of the ore freighter Nostromo landed on a barren planet to investigate a derelict spacecraft, found it filled with strange eggs, and unwittingly picked up the horrific life form that killed all but one of them. During those five decades, the barren world has been colonized, then ravaged by aliens. After being rescued from hypersleep, sole survivor Ripley (Sigourney Weaver) is compelled to return to the planet with some 'tough guys', where they fight 'like guerrillas in a supremely hostile territory' before ultimately blowing up the world and all its nasty inhabitants.

**RIGHT:** *Alien* star Sigourney Weaver as Ripley, a role she returned to in *Aliens* despite her reservations about all the film's gun-play.

**ABOVE:** Cameron pals Lance Henriksen (fourth from left) and Bill Paxton (second from right) as Bishop and Hudson respectively, in the iconic knife-game scene.

Having been 'stunned' by *Alien*, as well as helping to create its Corman-produced rip-off *Galaxy of Terror*, Cameron was hooked. But he maintained a poker face and simply said, 'That could be interesting.'

Over the following weeks, while *The Terminator* was paused and he was simultaneously scripting *Rambo* (see page 61), Cameron cooked up a treatment that took Hill and Giler's Ripley-plus-grunts concept and combined it with an idea of his own: an *Alien*-inspired story he had written a few years earlier titled *Mother* (previously

*E.T.*, until he saw that Steven Spielberg had used it). This involved a genetically engineered monster called a 'xenomorph' rampaging around a mining operation on Venus, and climaxed with its female lead character battling a xenomorph using a heavy-duty industrial power-suit exoskeleton, an idea he'd lifted from Robert A Heinlein's novel *Starship Troopers*, and already included in *Xenogenesis*.

The *Mother* character obviously became Ripley, whom Cameron had loved in the first film. 'She kind of emerged after everybody else got killed off,' he said. 'You didn't know she was the main character. . .I loved the unexpectedness of that. So, I wanted to get into her head more.' He gave her a backstory and a first name (Ellen), while placing her on a similar female-empowerment arc to *The Terminator*'s Sarah Connor, complete with its maternal undertones thanks to the introduction of a surrogate daughter in the form of nine-year-old colonist survivor Newt. This culminates in a face-to-face, power-suit-assisted battle against a deadly matriarch: the Alien (or xenomorph) Queen.

'What's bigger, meaner, more terrifying than the alien?' wrote Cameron in his treatment: 'Its mother'. Inspired by termites, he complemented (and completed) the life cycle imagined by *Alien* writers Dan O'Bannon and Ronald Shusett by answering the question of what laid those eggs, and visualized his own take on the nightmarish biomechanical creature designed for the original film by H R Giger. Cameron conceived her as 'a blend of what Giger does with what I wanted to do, which was to create something big and powerful and terrifying and female. Hideous and beautiful at the same time, like a black widow spider.' (Only 4 metres tall, and with acid for blood.)

While Ripley was his focus – to the extent that he would refuse to make a sequel that did not include her – Cameron had also been itching to see a 'military in the future' movie ever since reading Heinlein's book, which depicted an interstellar war between

humans and giant-bug aliens (and was eventually adapted into a hyper-satirical Paul Verhoeven film in 1997). Now he could achieve that himself, and weave in some recent historical relevance. 'It was a definite parallel to Vietnam,' he said of his script. 'The story of a technologically superior military force that is defeated by a determined, furtive, asymmetric enemy.' Where John Rambo would finally get to win in Cameron's parallel writing project, the colonial marines were, more accurately, destined to lose.

However, by the time he had completed *The Terminator* – whose success ensured him a directorial as well as a screenwriting role on the film he had cleverly retitled *Aliens* – Cameron was well aware that the project put him on 'dangerous ground'. After only just making his mark with his own hit movie, he was going straight into something that would inevitably be compared with a sci-fi classic from a well-respected director. Veteran producer Julia Phillips warned Cameron that anything good about *Aliens* would be attributed to Scott, and anything bad about it blamed on *him*. But he is not someone who easily suffers cold feet. This was the ultimate filmmaking challenge. 'How do you beat a classic?' he asked himself. 'You have to do a proper homage to the original without being a mindless fan: something that is a piece of entertainment and a story in its own right.'

The homage came in directly continuing Ripley's story (albeit after a youth-preserving 57-year hypersleep), building out her universe, and retaining *Alien*'s grimy, blue-collar vision of our extra-planetary future – a look that chimed well with Cameron's own tech-noir style. The distinction came in shifting genres from a stalker-horror film with a novel setting ('In space no one can hear

**LEFT:** Vasquez was the first-ever film role for Jenette Goldstein (right). She would appear in minor roles in two other Cameron movies: *Terminator 2* and *Titanic*.

**ABOVE:** Mark Rolston as Smartgun operator Drake, falling foul of the xenomorphs' acid blood.

you scream') to a war/siege movie with horror elements. Cameron was quick to point out the differences between himself and Ridley Scott. 'I probably gravitate more towards heavier plotting,' he said in 1986, with 'a little more concentration on characters and dialogue – and much more action – and less on the visual aspects.'

It is telling that he spoke in terms of 'beating' rather than matching Scott's film; by his own admission, Cameron has always been prone to hubris. As it turned out, *Aliens would* beat *Alien* at the US box office – just – grossing some $6 million more than its predecessor's $79 million domestic take. And if its qualitative superiority is hotly debated by fans and critics, the fact that the debate even exists should speak volumes to its still-enduring creative brilliance. In retrospect, it seems bizarre that anyone should have warned Cameron off making *Aliens* as his follow-up to *The Terminator*. Although, if he had been able to see into his own future, he might have warned himself. *The Terminator* had been tough: an exacting, all-out sprint of a production. But for the most part he had been allowed to make it his way, with little resistance until the final leg. In contrast, on *Aliens*, to paraphrase the tag line Cameron himself wrote for the film, this time it was war.

Cameron's battles began before he even started shooting. First, he had to convince the studio to hire Sigourney Weaver, without whom his film could not exist. Weaver approved of Cameron's script, and how it gave her character 'much greater emotional content' than *Alien*. 'He'd fleshed out the character of Ripley', she said. 'He really captured her, and made her this renegade.' As an anti-gun campaigner, she was concerned about the prominence of firearms in the story, but had sufficient faith in the director to commit regardless – once 20th Century Fox agreed to pay her what she felt she deserved for Ripley's comeback. Yet the studio kept resisting this, believing the film could be rewritten without Ripley, causing Cameron and Hurd (who was producing at Cameron's insistence) to threaten to quit over the matter.

In the end, Cameron came up with a 'ploy', he claimed, to finally get Weaver on board. He called up Arnold Schwarzenegger's agent Lou Pitt, who worked at the same firm as Weaver's agent, and told him that he had decided to drop Ripley, the only character from the first film (other than the cat), as a way of making the sequel '100 per cent mine'. As he had hoped, Pitt related this to Weaver's agent, who panicked and jumped on the phone to Fox, and within a day the deal was finally made – for a then astonishing (for an actress) $1 million. 'It was a close call,' said Cameron.

The downside of the deal was that it redoubled Fox's efforts to keep costs as low as possible, with the budget set at a relatively tight $18 million. This necessitated shooting the movie in England (cheaper than the United States) at Pinewood Studios with a largely British crew, and drawing most of the cast from the US expat acting community in the United Kingdom. This included unknowns like Jenette Goldstein (as tough Latina Vasquez), Mark Rolston (as the burly Drake) and William Hope (as inexperienced Lieutenant Gorman), as well as Carrie Henn, the 10-year-old daughter of a USAF pilot stationed in RAF Lakenheath, as Newt. Cameron was able to bring some pals along: Lance Henriksen took the role of the surprisingly non-malevolent android Bishop, and Texan actor Bill Paxton, whom Cameron had befriended at New World Pictures while painting sets, and had a tiny role as a spike-haired punk in *The Terminator*. As the wise-ass, panicky Hudson, he became one of the film's most beloved and quoted characters ('Game over, man. Game over!')

The role of smarmy Company man Burke went, in a smartly counterintuitive move, to comedian Paul Reiser, while the key marine role of Corporal Hicks was won by James Remar, veteran of a few Walter Hill movies, including *The Warriors*. Unfortunately, a few weeks into filming, Remar was, the actor admitted years later, 'busted for possession of drugs', and deported to the United States. So, Hurd and Cameron parachuted in Michael Biehn. He was a little concerned about the similarities between Hicks and Kyle Reese, both being soulful soldiers, but happy to be working again with his *Terminator* director.

Far less happy, by all accounts, were the British crew. While Cameron had a significant American contingent on his team – including trusted collaborators Stan Winston, who oversaw the creation of the awesome Alien Queen puppet, and FX experts Dennis and Robert Skotak – the majority of his crew were locals.

**ABOVE:** Ten-year-old unknown Carrie Henn was cast as Newt for her 'soulful' expressiveness, as Cameron put it. She chose not to continue her acting career after the movie.

Many were unconvinced that this cocky 'Yank upstart' (who some derisively called 'Grizzly Adams') was worthy of following in Ridley Scott's footsteps, and did not believe Hurd – a *woman,* and the director's wife, too – was capable of producing a film. 'People kept saying, "Who's really producing this movie?"', Hurd recalled. 'It was really difficult for me to maintain a sense of calm.'

**ABOVE:** Henriksen as Bishop, memorably torn in half by the Alien Queen during the film's rousing climax.

But the worst clashes were with Cameron. His cinematographer, Dick Bush, was fired after refusing to light a sequence as the director had requested, and replaced by Adrian Biddle. Cameron also fired assistant director Derek Cracknell after he rubbed up the cast the wrong way ('He kept calling me "love" and "sweetheart"', complained Goldstein of the cockney crewman), only re-hiring him after the whole crew downed tools and Weaver brokered a resolution.

Much of the friction was the result of transatlantic culture clash, but it was clear that a set-in-their-ways crew and a laser-focused, meticulous and often abrasive Cameron did not make for a good mix. 'Jim is a passionate, hard-driving type of a guy and could be insensitive to people's needs if they got in the way of making the movie that he wanted to make,' said Biehn – one of his biggest allies. It hardly helped that, thanks to Weaver getting held up on another production (*Half Moon Street*), Cameron's carefully planned schedule had been wrecked, and he was battling the clock, it seemed, every moment of every day.

One morning, his frustrations boiled over when yet another shot was delayed by the arrival of Pinewood's tea lady, causing the atmospheric set smoke to billow out through the door she had opened, and the crew to flock to her. Fuming, Cameron charged over and kicked her snack trolley, sending buns flying. 'Ah, the tea lady,' he said many years later. 'She was just caught at that terrible interface between these two cultures.' But his retrospective frustration at working in the United Kingdom persisted over the decades. 'The pace was about half the speed we were used to,' he reflected in 2008. 'It was like just going from running to running through gelatin.'

*Aliens* was a testing experience, across the board. 'Any Jim Cameron movie is a tough atmosphere,' admitted Winston in 1986. And this was the largest effects film he'd ever been part of; 'I can't think of any one, historically, that has its scope'. Weaver, meanwhile, pulled a ligament in her back early in the shoot, and later struggled with her action scenes, 'running up and down the stairs with lit flamethrowers' at the film's only location, a recently decommissioned power station in Acton, West London (which had to undergo extensive asbestos removal, causing further delays). 'You have to be terribly careful that you reach for the right button,' Weaver said of her incendiary prop, 'so you don't accidentally flame somebody. The physical responsibility was huge.'

There were mishaps, too. While shooting the processing station escape sequence, where the majority of the ensemble is thrillingly eliminated by the first xenomorph strike, the actors found themselves literally starved of air by the intensity of the too-close-for-comfort FX flames. 'They pulled us out. They had to give us oxygen. They sent us to lunch,' remembered Paxton. Then, while filming the dropship landing sequence, the APC (armoured personnel carrier) set was rocked so hard by the crew that its roof collapsed. 'It grazed Sigourney and I think it hit William Hope,' recalled Rolston. 'It was a scary moment.'

The struggles over *Aliens* did not end with principal photography. So much time had been lost that composer James Horner (who had provided some rousing themes for *Battle Beyond the Stars*) only had 10 days to write his score, when he had been expecting six weeks. 'They didn't know what they were asking; how inhuman and how difficult it was,' said Horner, who would not work again with Cameron until *Titanic* 11 years later. But he somehow pulled it off, and the results remain energizingly bombastic.

Cameron was also forced by the studio to cut his 154-minute film down to two hours, to maximize the number of its daily showings. After wrestling with the edit, the director insisted that he could go no shorter than 137 minutes. If he cut any more, he said, 'the movie wouldn't make sense.' Fox reluctantly accepted this, especially as there was no time for any test screenings. The studio was suitably relieved when *Aliens* proved to be a hit, regardless.

As the film was, like *The Terminator*, calibrated to be a thrill-ride first and foremost, it was not to some critics' tastes. The *New York Times*' Walter Goodman was particularly savage, writing, 'The effects, perils in outer space and in shadowy corners, quite overwhelm the skimpy script, which is loaded with gibberish uttered with authority.' *Variety*, meanwhile, compared Cameron

## Cameron's cut: *Aliens: Special Edition*

When *Aliens* was first broadcast on US television (by CBS) in 1989, some of its cut scenes were returned to extend its running time. These included the revelation that Ripley had a daughter who had died in her 60s during Ripley's long hypersleep – underscoring her maternal feelings towards Newt – and sequences involving automated sentry guns being set up and cutting down xenomorphs as they encroach en masse, thus emphasizing the species' relentless, swarm-like nature. But it was not until the laserdisc release in 1991 that Cameron was able to fully restore his original vision for the film.

The main sequence he had reluctantly excised to meet Fox's running-time demand was a visit to the Alien-world, LV-426 (aka Acheron), that takes place between the recovery of Ripley and the news that the Company has lost contact with the colony. After seeing the escape shuttle *Narcissus* at the opening of the film, this was the only moment to revisit a location from *Alien*, namely the derelict spacecraft where all the eggs were stored. This time, its visitors are salvage-seeking prospectors from the colony Hadley's Hope: Newt's parents, who have brought her and Timmy (played by Carrie Henn's brother Christopher) along for the ride. So, rather coincidentally, the first time we glimpse a parasitic facehugger, it is from Newt's perspective, screaming as she sees it clasped to her dad's head.

While there is some connective value to showing the derelict spacecraft, revealing the colony before Ripley and the marines arrive dilutes the tension somewhat. The film is more subjectively effective when we find Hadley's Hope as Ripley finds it: this chilling ghost town, where just one feral girl survives and unseen monsters lurk. The cut, then, was a smart one. However, the other restituted scenes are more welcome, including a memorable speech from Bill Paxton's Hudson, in which he brags about all the kick-ass hardware the marines are packing, including, he jokes, 'sharp sticks'.

The Special Edition was such a success, it sparked a new industry trend for director's cuts. Cameron would put out extended versions of his next two films and *Avatar*, but funnily enough it is *Alien* director Ridley Scott who's got the most mileage out of the fad, putting out 'Extended' or 'Director's' cuts of 11 of his films to date.

unfavourably with Ridley Scott. 'The overall impression is of a film made by an expert craftsman,' it read, 'while Scott clearly had something of an artist in him.'

However, the audience begged to differ, with *Aliens* becoming the fifth biggest movie at the US box office that year and earning seven Oscar nominations, including Best Actress for Weaver. 'It was so unusual for the Academy to recognize a science-fiction, fantasy and horror film,' noted Paxton. Its popularity has only grown over the

**ABOVE:** The mother of all sci-fi battles: Ripley takes on the Alien Queen using a powerloader exoskeleton suit.

years; in 2023, *Variety* announced it as one of the 'Best movie sequels of all time', while the following year, a documentary on the movie, *Aliens Expanded,* spent a remarkable 4 hours and 42 minutes reverently exploring its production and impact. 'Without a doubt, it is my love letter to Cameron's finest film,' said writer-director Ian Nathan.

As with *The Terminator*, Cameron himself is a harsh judge, stating, 'In terms of actual technique, it's crude compared to the films that are made now.' But, he added, 'in terms of storytelling, it's as good as I'll ever be.' He is half-right, there. It is hard to imagine the Alien Queen having greater presence and more hissing, chilling menace if she were rendered with CGI rather than Winston's ingenious puppetry. For all its budgetary limitations, the film's miniature models, stark sets, relatable-future design and immersively subjective camera work still hold up, and still match the breathtaking, 'express elevator to Hell' ride of its narrative.

Against the odds, Cameron had crafted an action sci-fi masterpiece. For most other directors, an experience like *Aliens* would be a career one-off: an intense test of their abilities (and sanity) that they would hope never to repeat. For Cameron, however, it was just the start of a long, painful journey into filmmaking extremity.

*'It's a bottomless pit, baby'*

# THE ABYSS
## 1989

**T**he *Abyss* was very nearly James Cameron's last movie. Because making *The Abyss* very nearly killed him.

Cameron's alien-visitation thriller is set, for the most part, in an undersea oil rig on the ocean floor at the edge of the Cayman Trough, where bioluminescent 'NTIs' (non-terrestrial intelligences) dwell far below human reach. As the director insisted on shooting 'wet for wet' to create this extreme environment, he, his crew and all the actors spent most of the production in a water-filled containment vessel at the never-completed Cherokee Nuclear Power Plant near Gaffney, South Carolina. It was the only tank in the world big enough to accommodate Cameron's ambitious vision: the largest underwater set ever built. An accomplished diver, he was able to spend the long working days mostly underwater, in a custom-made 18 kg helmet (designed to fully reveal the wearer's face and allow them to speak), with weights on his waist and ankles to keep him anchored, 10 metres down, at the bottom of the tank. As his air tanks only held enough oxygen for about 75 minutes, there was an air-filling station down there, too, so filming would not be constantly delayed by people needing to decompress and refill above water. However, Cameron needed his assistant director to remind him when each hour passed, as he was often too absorbed in the minutiae of filming to notice his pressure gauge dropping.

One day, his AD forgot. Cameron suddenly realized he could not breathe. His pressure gauge was at zero. Nobody was nearby. He announced on his comm system that he was in trouble. Nobody responded. Every second counted, so he decided to get himself to the surface as quickly as possible. He stripped off his helmet – and with it the buoyancy vest to which it was attached – and began blindly ascending, kicking hard to counter the weights, breathing out as he went to prevent his compressed-air-filled lungs exploding as the pressure suddenly dropped.

**ABOVE:** Like all the cast of *The Abyss*, Mary Elizabeth Mastrantonio (as Dr Lindsey Brigman) had to spend long days shooting underwater.

Finally, one of the production's safety divers spotted his distress. However, he did not see that Cameron was attempting to equalize as he thrashed his way upwards, so he halted the director's progress about halfway there and rammed an emergency backup regulator into Cameron's mouth. But the regulator was not working. He inhaled water instead of air and started choking. With no way to communicate this to the safety diver, who was holding him fast, assuming Cameron was panicking, he punched the poor guy in the face and managed to reach the surface just before he blacked out.

THE ABYSS

It was a close call. But he was back in the water the next day, continuing the shoot…after firing both his AD and the safety diver.

*The Abyss* has gone down in movie-making history as one of the most difficult and dangerous films ever produced in Hollywood. It also, with some justification, sealed Cameron's reputation for being a tyrannical director. But, as his near-death experience reveals, nobody was ever in any doubt that Cameron himself was willing to work at least as hard, and take at least as many risks, as anyone he hired.

After the success of *Aliens*, 20th Century Fox was keen to stay in the James Cameron business, so gave him the closest Hollywood ever gets to a blank cheque for his next movie. But the director was in no rush to dive back behind a camera, and announced at the time that he had '10 ideas' he was working up, while his partner Gale Anne Hurd pursued her own new project: a satirical sci-fi take on the mismatched-cop genre titled *Alien Nation*. In the end, with Hurd's encouragement, the idea he settled on was the oldest, a story he had written way back in 1970 as a bored high-schooler.

Titled *The Abyss* (after the famous Friedrich Nietzsche quote, 'if you gaze long enough into an abyss, the abyss will gaze back into you'), it involved a group of deep-sea scientists encountering highly advanced subaquatic aliens who, in a briny twist on sci-fi classic *The Day The Earth Stood Still*, intend to punish humanity for its warlike and rapacious ways – until they are dissuaded by the film's deep-diving human hero. The young Cameron had broadly been inspired to locate his sci-fi story in the sea rather than space by the TV documentaries of French oceanographer Jacques Cousteau. But what really catalysed the concept was a school trip to a science exhibition in Buffalo, New York. Here, one lecturer revealed the existence of liquid oxygen, which in theory would enable people to dive deeper than ever before. Except it only

**ABOVE:** Todd Graff as oil-rig worker Hippy, with one of the five rats who played his rodent pal Beany.

worked on small animals, like lab rats – which ultimately included the five that Cameron cast in *The Abyss* as crew rat Beany, whom he would film breathing the puce fluid for real in a scene that had to be cut for the UK release due to animal welfare concerns.

In Cameron's final screenplay for *The Abyss*, the scientists were switched up for ruggedly loveable oil workers, swapping white coats for blue collars to make them more relatable to the audience. To add tension, he had their high-tech, ocean-bed rig sequestered by Navy SEALs (led by Michael Biehn, now in moustachioed bad-guy mode) on a mission to rescue a nuclear submarine neutralized by the NTIs, and worked in a ticking-clock element via an incoming hurricane. More significantly, at the movie's heart he placed a married couple, Bud and Lindsey Brigman (Ed Harris and Mary Elizabeth Mastrantonio) who, just to add some emotional sparks, are undergoing a divorce.

Around the time of writing the script, Cameron's own marriage was starting to fall apart. The director has since insisted that the screenplay was completed before he and Gale Anne Hurd separated, so it could only have been coincidental. 'If it paralleled the situation,' he said, 'it may have only been a kind of sub-subconscious anxiety about separation in general.' If so, that anxiety surfaces on screen in one discomfiting way. While Lindsey certainly fits the Cameron 'strong female lead character' mould, she is also repeatedly described as a 'bitch' in the film; when we first see her striding purposefully across a ship's deck, one character groans and calls her 'the Queen Bitch of the Universe'. As it turns out, Lindsey is simply highly capable and understandably uncompromising in a shit-talking, male-dominated environment. Rather like Hurd. But the multiple uses of the slur do start to smack of vitriol on Cameron's part, and give the film a taint of misogyny.

Still, it says much about his professional faith in Hurd that he wanted her on board, despite their personal situation. 'We were separated pending a divorce when I asked her to produce *The Abyss*,' he recalled. 'I went to her and said, "Look, this is going to be really hard on us. We're going to get dragged over a cheese grater when this film comes out. But I think you should produce it."' As it turned out, the implications of their marital situation would be the least of their worries on this shoot.

'I'm James Cameron,' the director announces to the behind-the-scenes camera during principal photography for *The Abyss*. He is deep underwater in that heavy face-revealing helmet, his voice distorted by the comms system that will enable the film to be the

## Cameron's cut: *The Abyss: Special Edition*

Cameron had long suffered a recurring nightmare, of 'a vast wave rolling towards the shore, miles high, turning day into night.' So this became the method by which the NTIs of *The Abyss* would execute humanity for its crimes, and Cameron tasked VFX outfit ILM with conjuring it up, using footage of real waves shot by surfing photographer Yuri Farrant in Hawaii.

Yet, despite all this effort, the wave was cut from *The Abyss*. The studio insisted that two hours and 51 minutes was far too long for a big summer movie and, as Cameron said, 'I've always found that the easiest way to radically reduce a picture is to remove an entire subplot, not pick away at it. So the wave sequence was a really good candidate for me.' Especially as half the film's test audience said the sequence – prefaced by the aliens pointedly showing Bud historical images of human atrocity, from the Holocaust to mushroom clouds – felt out of place.

However, Cameron would later rue his decision. 'I made cuts to the film I shouldn't have made,' he said. 'I believe we misinterpreted the results [of the test screening], due to my inexperience.' Still, as with *Aliens*, he was eventually able to share his original vision via a Special Edition home-entertainment release, with the 3,000-metre-high wave and his tribute to *The Day The Earth Stood Still* back in place. Though it would take the success of his next film, *Terminator 2*, to finally convince the studio it was worth the effort and expense.

first to ever record subaquatic dialogue. 'I want to take you into a world of cold, darkness and unrelenting pressure,' he continues. 'The movie business!'

He knew it would be tough. Unlike depictions of space travel, which for the most part ignore the absence of gravity, this could not be faked. He warned his cast before they signed on. 'If you're claustrophobic, don't like water and are not prepared to work harder than you've ever worked in your life, don't take part,' he said.

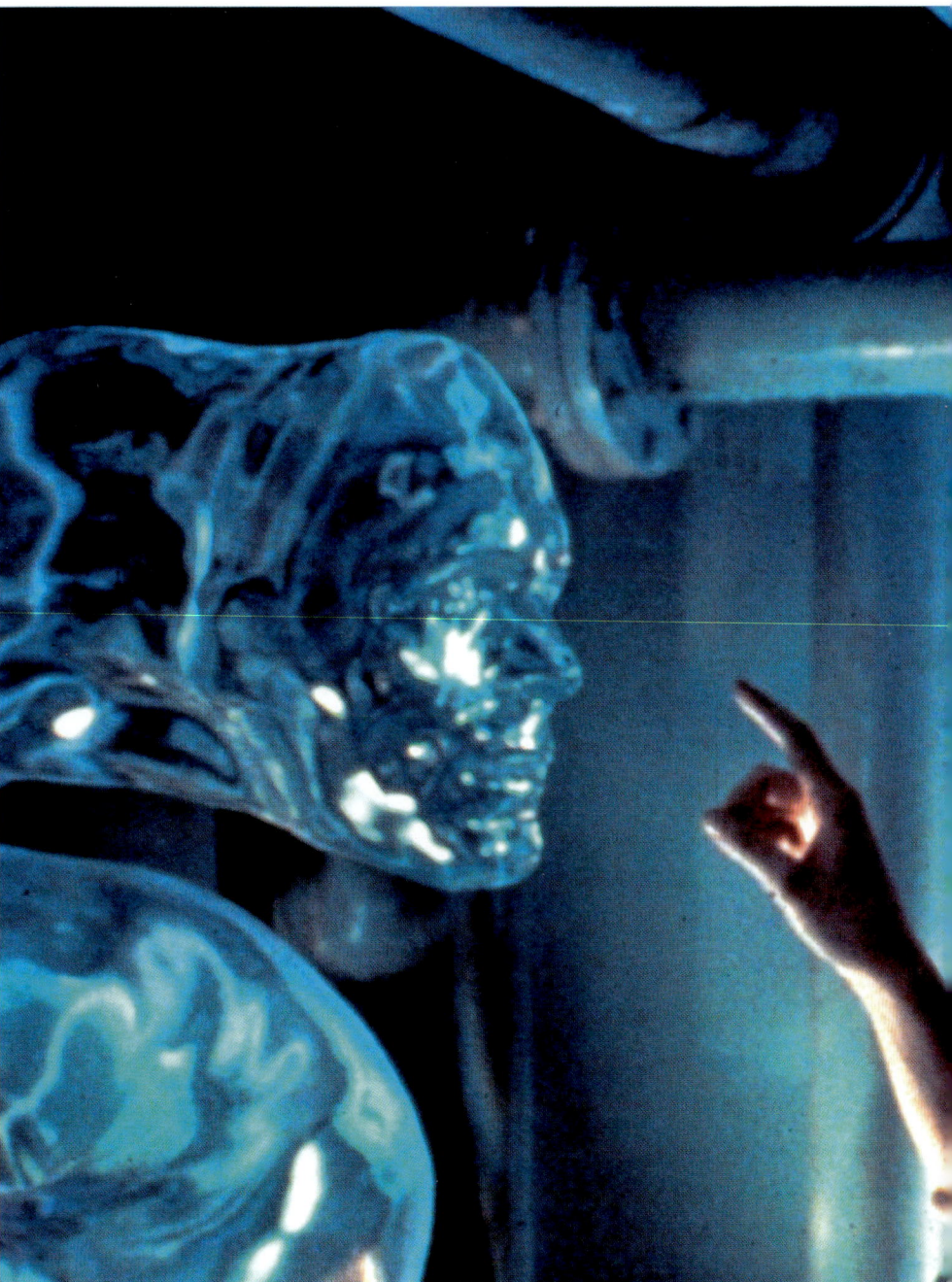

Everyone underwent weeks of scuba-diving training, with repeated bail-out drills. Yet for most of those involved, making *The Abyss* – or 'The Abuse' as some renamed it – was far harder than they ever could have expected. 'On the first day of shooting,' remembered actor Leo Burmester (who plays loveable roughneck Catfish De Vries), 'Jim looks at us and says, "Hello boys. Welcome to my nightmare".' It was one he shared with everybody.

Harris, cast as Bud for his rugged demeanour rather than his star power, had to perform extended scenes while holding his breath. Towards the end of the film, Bud is immersed in helmet-filling liquid oxygen, so he can descend the Trough and defuse a nuclear warhead dropped down there by Biehn's SEAL, Coffey, who's lost his mind to pressure sickness. But with humans still unable to survive in liquid oxygen, Harris had to fake it. During one long take, he realized he just could not hold his breath any longer. The fluid started going up his nostrils. He needed air fast. Sure enough, one of the safety divers reached him with a regulator, but accidentally applied it upside-down. 'I got a lot of water in my lungs,' Harris recalled. 'For a split second I thought I was a goner.'

Fortunately, underwater director of photography Al Giddings, a veteran of movies like *The Deep* and *For Your Eyes Only*, saw what was happening and came to the rescue with his own respirator. Even so, Harris was deeply shaken. 'I really thought I was going to die for a second, and it pissed me off that I was afraid of that. Though it never got that dangerous again, I had to be in that suit until the last day of shooting. I always knew I was going to have to go back down in this fucking fluid-breathing suit.'

**PREVIOUS PAGE:** Lindsey and Bud (Ed Harris) encounter the 'pseudopod', a groundbreaking digital effect created by ILM.

**LEFT:** Harris wasn't an actor who typically got lead roles, but he had the rugged quality Cameron required for Bud.

As well as the expected cold, discomfort and long waiting times between scene re-sets during the 15- to 18-hour days, there was also an accidental over-chlorination of the water, which caused stinging eyes and bleached hair. Plus, to prevent surface reflections ruining shots, it was covered in tiny black plastic beads, which irritatingly got into every fold and crevice on the cast and crew's bodies. Sometimes the water got too cloudy to shoot in, thanks to problems with the filtration system; or, at one time, as the result of soluble glue being used to adhere some set elements. Or, at another time, the unwelcome arrival of some local goats, who urinated in the tank.

'We realized from the beginning that it was going to be difficult,' said Hurd. 'What we didn't realize was that it was actually going to be impossible. In the sense that we never really got things under control.' To Cameron, this was the inherent nature of the enterprise. 'It was just one thing after another,' he said. 'But the enormity of this undertaking never discouraged me. If anything, it encouraged me.'

Cameron's focus, his demands, and his lack of sympathy created friction with his performers. While publicizing the film, they aired their frustration at the long stretches of waiting underwater. 'You know, life's a bitch,' Cameron snarled in response. 'I shed not one single tear for them, because all the hours they're waiting, the crew is busting their backs. Poor babies.' Even staunch ally Biehn described him as being 'often insensitive to actors of Ed and Mary's class.'

During the shooting of an especially exacting sequence, Mastrantonio snapped. After their submersible is irreparably damaged during a kinetic vehicular confrontation with Coffey, Lindsey voluntarily drowns, in the slim hope that Bud – the better swimmer, with the only air supply between them – can revive her on returning to base. What follows is a long, uncomfortable,

**ABOVE:** The infamous resuscitation scene, which pushed Mastrantonio to the limit.

emotionally intense scene where the distraught Bud and his surviving crew try to bring her back, tearing open her shirt and using CPR. They think they have failed and lost her, before Bud furiously pummels the 'bitch' back into consciousness. During the first take, Harris' arm accidentally blocked Mastrantonio's pallid, blue-lipped face during a crucial moment. But the actors nailed it on the second take – until the camera ran out of film just as Lindsey started to resurrect. This was too much for the actress, who by now had spent hours lying, chest exposed, on a freezing cold grill. 'We're not animals here!' she screamed at Cameron, and stormed off the set.

'I understand the pressure and how it got to her,' the director admitted years later. 'It was our fault.' Even so, Mastrantonio said, 'Before [the shoot] was over I'd want to kill him at least a dozen times.'

Of course, Cameron nearly did that to himself. And while it did not excuse his occasional flares of temper or – as actor Todd Graff (who played conspiracy-nut rig worker Hippy) put it, his bad 'bedside manner' – Cameron reportedly exerted himself more than anybody else on the production. Indeed, he put in so many daily hours underwater, he needed to decompress for an hour at the close of each day; time he spent upside-down (to relieve the weight of his helmet) reviewing footage from the previous day's filming. 'I was stunned by Jim's allegiance to the project and the extent of his physical abilities,' said Giddings. 'It was beyond belief his commitment to what we were doing.'

Cameron's achievement went further than physical exertion. Enlisting the help of his brother Mike (now a mechanical engineer), he earned five cinematic equipment patents while making the film. First, he and Mike invented The SeaWasp, a camera-propulsion vehicle that provided smooth underwater movement. Then there were the full-face masks (meaning actors' faces could be seen by the audience) and their comms system (which allowed Cameron to speak to the actors, but not them to speak back). And there was that underwater oxygen station, too. He also, more famously, engendered a visual effects breakthrough.

Many of the VFX were achieved, under visual effects supervisor Steve Johnson, using traditional techniques. These included scale models (shot in a second, smaller tank), rear projection, optical effects or puppetry for the manta ray/jellyfish/angel-like NTIs – all of which were complicated massively by the demands of shooting

**RIGHT:** *The Abyss'* impressive underwater scenes were all shot in an unfinished nuclear power plant.

CHAPTER FIVE

**ABOVE:** Bud's oil-rig crew included Leo Burmester (left) as Catfish, and John Bedford Lloyd (centre) as Jammer.

underwater. However, new technology was required for the scene in which Lindsey, Bud and co have a close encounter with the 'pseudopod', as Cameron called it: a tendril of apparently living water that can replicate the characters' faces. For this, Dennis Muren of George Lucas' VFX company Industrial Light and Magic (ILM) stepped forward. Building on 'morphing' techniques ILM had just developed for Ron Howard's fantasy flop *Willow* (which allowed a character to smoothly shapeshift between a variety of animal forms), Muren was able to use computer-generated imagery to manifest Cameron's watery tentacle. For the first time, CGI presented something convincingly organic, rather than bearing the sheen of artifice. It took ILM nine months to deliver 20 shots, but the results were spectacular. On release, critic Kim Newman described the pseudopod as an 'absolutely magical alien special effect.'

**ABOVE:** At the end of the film, the strong, independent Lindsey falls once more for her estranged husband Bud.

An expensive one, too. But that was just a drop in the ocean for a movie whose total costs were reported as being between $43 and $47 million, and have since been estimated as closer to $70 million. The film's budget, the shoot's troubles and the fact that it overran – necessitating a release-date delay of over a month – dominated press coverage. The *Los Angeles Times* almost gleefully pointed out that, while other studios raked it in with summer hits like *Batman*, *Lethal Weapon 2* and *Indiana Jones and the Last Crusade*, Fox was 'waiting with mounting exasperation' for Cameron to deliver, while wringing its hands 'over studio money plummeting into a bottomless abyss.' However, the same article does emphasize that Cameron himself lost out as a result, thanks to much of his salary being contractually forfeited to cover the overruns. 'Meaning I worked for half price,' the director stated.

Frustratingly for Cameron, and for Fox, all the blood, sweat, tears and goat's piss did not quite pay off. Released late in blockbuster season, and with a long running time of two hours and 20 minutes (even after extensive cuts), the movie only grossed just over $52 million in the United States, eventually making $90 million worldwide – not the biggest of profit margins.

Reviews were mixed, too. While Cameron's aptitude for action, tension-building and pushing the FX envelope was deservedly recognized (the movie won an Oscar for its VFX), its final-act diversion into wishy-washy alien-encounter territory stumped many viewers. Not least because the whole humanity-judging element had wound up on the cutting-room floor during a tense and rushed edit. This leaves the NTIs' intentions irksomely oblique, even after they kindly rescue Bud, Lindsey and all their pals, returning them safely to the surface in a gigantic, opalescent swimming-saucer. This, wrote *Newsweek*'s critic David Ansen, is a 'pretty damn silly [and] portentous *deus ex machina* that leaves too many questions unanswered and evokes too many other films'. Cameron's dubious treatment of Lindsey – who, in the end, falls for Bud all over again – was also brought up by Rita Kempley of *The Washington Post*. The film, she said, 'asks us to believe that the drowned return to life, that the comatose come to the rescue, that driven women become doting wives. . .I'd sooner believe that Moby Dick could swim up the drainpipe.'

*The Abyss* remains a frustrating viewing experience. At its best, it is claustrophobically gripping. Nobody had ever shot underwater scenes so effectively before. But its ending sits awkwardly, even with its extra scenes restituted in the Special Edition (see page 89). 'It seems like you're in a completely different movie for the last chunk of it,' said Graff. 'When did it become *E.T.!*?'

In extra-terrestrial terms, Cameron had gone from demons in *Aliens* to angels in *The Abyss*, who not only spare humanity but

**ABOVE:** For the scenes where Bud inhales liquid oxygen, Harris (centre left) had to hold his breath for long periods.

also heal marriages. The film, rather cheesily, ends with a kiss. This was the first sign of a sentimentality that would seep steadily into Cameron's work from this point onwards. But while, in *The Abyss*, it did not quite gel with the preceding high-pressure thrills, in his later work it would start striking chords with audiences in massively successful ways. Starting with a movie that, somewhat improbably, would turn his biggest villain into his greatest hero.

*'All you know how to create
is death and destruction'*

# TERMINATOR 2: JUDGMENT DAY
## 1991

Late on 5 November 1990, a crowd of around 200 people gathered in Fremont, a suburb of San Jose, California. Some had brought chairs to sit on, while others perched with binoculars on bales of hay that someone had offloaded from their pickup truck. It was a cold and damp night, but many of the enthusiastic throng were warming themselves with flasks of coffee.

Then, in the three-story office building across the street, the fireworks started: Arnold Schwarzenegger (or possibly his stunt double Peter Kent – no one was close enough to be sure) appeared at a blown-out window on the second floor. Clad in Terminator leather and wielding a huge helicopter mini-gun, he started blasting, and the police cars and SWAT vans in the car park below began exploding in response, sending glass and cop-uniformed

**ABOVE:** The newer, kinder Terminator (Arnold Schwarzenegger) in the Cyberdyne parking lot scene. He still uses heavy weaponry, but non-lethally.

stuntmen flying. When the dust settled, the smoke cleared and the cameras stopped rolling, the crowd whooped with joy.

It had not been like this on the set of *The Terminator*, seven years earlier. The only members of the public who had gathered during that shoot were a queue of hopeful nightclubbers who mistook Tech-Noir for a real-deal establishment. Where that production had gone under the radar, this one was the talk of the town. *Terminator 2: Judgment Day* had the biggest-ever budget for a movie, at a reported $100 million. It was packed with action – around 60 per cent of its running time, its stunt coordinator estimated – that largely played out on California's streets and freeways. It was the long-awaited sequel to a movie that had, since its release, permeated popular culture. It would, its makers promised, revolutionize visual effects. And it was fronted by an actor who, since making his mark in the original film, had become the world's biggest star: Arnold Schwarzenegger. As he always promised, he was back. And unafraid to feed the hype.

'I have to say that I feel sorry for the movie industry in a way,' Schwarzenegger told *Empire* magazine during the shoot. 'Because from this movie on, they're going to be screwed. Where else can they go?

This is it. This is the answer, and these poor studio executives are sitting out there trying to figure out how to top it. And you know what? They can't!'

After *The Abyss*, James Cameron was in dire need of a hit. As *Entertainment Weekly* suggested at the time, his follow-up 'could be the last big-budget movie he ever directs'. He was doing well in other areas of his life, having set up his own production company Lightstorm Entertainment, and he had also recently fallen for and swiftly married *Blue Steel* director Kathryn Bigelow, whose action hit *Point Break* he produced and script-doctored in 1991. But Cameron was well aware that if his next film stumbled, he might be finished as an A-list director.

A sequel to *The Terminator* would have seemed the safest bet. Especially as Schwarzenegger had been keen to do it for years, bringing it up whenever he and Cameron spoke. However, Cameron did not have the rights. Those still lay with Gale Anne Hurd, now his ex, and Hemdale Film Corporation, whom he refused to work with again. But then, serendipity struck.

Just before Christmas 1989, Cameron received a phone call from Carolco Pictures boss Mario Kassar, who had recently cast Schwarzenegger in action-sci-fi mindbender *Total Recall*. The Beirut-born producer revealed that his company had just bought the rights to *The Terminator* from Hurd and Hemdale, and that he wanted Cameron to direct the sequel. 'We'll pay you $6 million,' said Kassar. 'You have my full attention,' replied Cameron. It was, he later said, 'a ridiculous amount of money at that point in time.' So it was a short conversation; he could, he joked, 'be bought'. Though there was one complication: Carolco wanted the movie to be released on 3 July 1991, meaning he would have to start on the script immediately, and would have a very tight schedule (roughly the same as *Aliens*) to turn the whole thing around.

## The mini-sequel: *T2 3D: Battle Across Time* (1996)

Since *Judgment Day*, there have been four cinematic *Terminator* sequels, plus TV shows *The Sarah Connor Chronicles* (2008–09) and *Terminator Zero* (2024). But in May 1995, Cameron himself returned to direct Arnold Schwarzenegger, Linda Hamilton, Edward Furlong and Robert Patrick in a follow-up adventure. It was 'actually a continuation of the storyline,' Cameron said, which sends John Connor and a Terminator into the Future War to blow up Skynet, and deal with a gigantic liquid-metal monster called, rather ridiculously, the T-1000000. It was never seen in cinemas.

*T2 3D: Battle Across Time* was an attraction launched at Universal Studios Florida in 1996, which blended live stunt performances and impressive stagecraft with Cameron's elaborate 3D screen-work, projected onto a triptych of screens. The state-of-the-art show was so successful, it also opened at Universal Studios in Hollywood and Japan, and ran for over 11 years at its original location (going for a further three years in Osaka).

Fortunately, Cameron had a reliable friend in William Wisher, with whom he collaborated on the screenplay. Plus, the sequel's central idea was already in place. 'Jim pulled this old yellow sheet of paper out of a notebook,' Wisher remembered of their first meeting about the film. 'He handed it to me without saying anything. There was one sentence scribbled on the dog-eared page. It read: "Young John Connor and the Terminator that comes back to befriend him."'

As the movie's tagline went, 'He's back…for good'. The unstoppable killer from the first film would, in this second instalment, become an immovable protector: a new 'Model 101' (that is, Schwarzenegger-shaped), reprogrammed and sent 35 years back in time by human resistance leader John Connor to protect his 10-year-old self from a second, more advanced Terminator. It is an

inventive pivot, which gives the film much of its humour, heart and dramatic heft as the young tearaway Connor (played by complete newcomer Edward Furlong, a non-actor discovered by casting director Mali Finn) starts to teach his Terminator about the ways of humanity – beginning with a blanket ban on actually terminating people – and moulds him into an unlikely father figure. 'Sure there's going to be big, thunderous action sequences,' said Cameron, 'but the heart of the movie is that relationship. I have always loved *The Wizard of Oz*. This movie is about the Tin Man getting his heart.'

But Schwarzenegger did not get it. 'He hated the idea,' Cameron related. After reading the script, the star complained, 'I don't get to kill anybody!' That was what was so good about the concept, Cameron insisted. 'We take this guy who's this monster and we make him a hero!' It was important to the director that Schwarzenegger not simply repeat himself as another cyborg assassin. Partly to give this film a different texture to the first – less lean, less mean. But also to address something that had been bothering him as the first film had grown in popularity and, in tandem with *Rambo*, driven the trend for one-man-army action films – which often starred Schwarzenegger, before he started softening his image in comedies like *Twins*. When *The Terminator* came out, 'it was fine for Arnold to play an absolute lethal cold-blooded killer,' Cameron said in 1991. 'Now, though, his role globally has changed and he's a great idol to children and people everywhere.'

In the first movie, he and Schwarzenegger had come up with a villain people cheered for. In this one, Cameron was determined that they would turn that villain not only into a hero, but a character

**LEFT:** Edward Furlong as John Connor. Furlong had no previous acting experience, and was spotted by casting director Mali Finn at the Pasadena Boys Club in 1990.

who would even make the audience *cry* – when, after finally saving the day, this sensitive new Model 101 sacrifices itself to stop its future-tech falling into the wrong hands. The aim, Cameron said, was to make a film 'about the value of human life'. Even if it took a reprogrammed killer robot to make us appreciate it.

Schwarzenegger, of course, came round, and by the time they started shooting had embraced the concept. Indeed, *Terminator 2* is one of his finest performances, locating a sweet spot between his brutal action operas and his daft comedies, as he forms a touching double-trouble act with Furlong. (Cameron often had to berate the pair for clowning around together between takes.) While still all brawn and chrome-hearted glare, the ghost in this particular machine is a glimmer of childlike innocence that Schwarzenegger allows to glow gradually brighter as the robot learns from John. Which is not to say *Judgment Day* entirely succumbs to schmaltz. Aside from the fact that John's Terminator occasionally maims people for audience laughs ('He'll live,' he says, after shooting an innocent security guard in the leg), it has plenty of hard edges.

Ironically, in this film, Sarah Connor is more of a Terminator than the guy who played him in the first film. The returning Linda Hamilton underwent one of the most remarkable physical transformations ever made by an actor between films. She turned the bouffant teen waitress into a sinewy, single-minded combat machine, whose focus on apocalyptic survival and Cassandra-like obsession with the incoming day of nuclear reckoning has driven her into a mental institution.

Hamilton was keen to make Sarah 'crazy' in this movie, and Cameron was more than happy to oblige, forging a very different brand of strong-female lead to Ripley in *Aliens*. 'Ripley's been through a trauma, but she had certain innate characteristics of

**ABOVE:** Linda Hamilton trained intensively to turn Sarah Connor into a convincing survivalist warrior.

leadership and wisdom under fire,' said Cameron. 'Sarah's not really a hero. She's an ordinary person who's been put under extreme pressure, and that makes her warped and twisted, but at the same time strengthened, in a sad kind of way.'

In performance terms, the steely-but-dented Hamilton is easily the film's stand-out, especially once the story breaks from the chase format to follow Sarah's second-act mission to prevent Judgment Day by terminating Cyberdyne scientist Miles Dyson (Joe Morton). In a fun new tweak on the first film's time-loopiness, she discovers that he is on course to invent Skynet by reverse-engineering the remains of the original 1984 Terminator. (Meaning that if Sarah had not destroyed it, it may never have been created in the first place.) She decides he must die, and tracks him down to his family home where she comes close to murdering him in front of his wife and young son. 'She's gone cold. She's gone dark. She's become a machine,' said Cameron, who was hugely impressed in this sequence by how well Hamilton had responded to her combat training with ex-Israeli commando Uziel Gal. 'She trained so rigorously to be able to pull that off better than any guy in the fucking history of movies,' he said. 'She was terrifying.'

But she does not pull the trigger. In the end, she is not quite machine-like enough to erase one human life to theoretically save six billion others. Even though, as we see in a truly disturbing dream sequence, she suffers visions of those billions dying in an atomic conflagration, depicted via astonishing model work by the Skotak brothers, plus some distressing human-disintegration animatronics courtesy of Stan Winston.

Far less concerned by the value of a single human life is the film's true villain: the other Terminator, sent to kill John Connor. At an early stage in the writing process, Cameron and Wisher discussed a 'two-Arnold concept', which would have Schwarzenegger playing both robots. However, Cameron decided it felt too 'gimmicky' and would have required his star to spend more than double the time in make-up, to create two different looks. Still, to turn his hero cyborg into an underdog, he needed something 'bigger, stronger and more terrifying' than Schwarzenegger's 'T-800' Terminator.

Instead he went back to an idea he'd originally come up with, then abandoned, in early drafts for the first film: 'A sort of liquid metal robot that could take any form.' John Carpenter's *The Thing*, he felt at the time, beat him to the idea of a shape-changing monster, and he was not convinced early-80s visual effects were up to the task. But now ILM's success with the pseudopod in *The*

**ABOVE:** Robert Patrick made his acting breakthrough as the menacing T-1000.

**FOLLOWING PAGE:** The T-1000's exploded 'Pretzel Man' form was a practical effect created by the Stan Winston Studio.

*Abyss* suggested that it could be pulled off using CGI, whether this 'mimetic poly-alloy' was striding in human form, smoothly morphing itself into other identities, or reshaping its body parts into lethal weapons. ILM's Dennis Muren did not shy away from the challenge, even though it had taken nine months to render just 75 seconds of water-tentacle wonder. Here they would be creating a main character, doing things never before seen on screen. 'It

### Cameron's cut: *Terminator 2: Special Edition*

The Special Edition of *T2* runs 16 minutes longer, and is most notable for fleshing out the T-800's evolution towards emotionality, in a scene where the cyborg reveals it can be reprogrammed via the removal of a chip. The scene was complicated to shoot (requiring a fake mirror, a fully animatronic Arnold Schwarzenegger and Linda Hamilton's twin sister playing Sarah's reflection) and featured the heroine attempting to destroy the chip, before her son pleads for her to spare his new robotic friend. Later, John teaches the Terminator to smile (badly) in a scene that the film is better without. Also restored is a dream sequence that briefly returns Michael Biehn as Kyle Reese, to unsubtly remind Sarah that 'the future is not set'.

An even longer version of the film is included as a hidden extra on the 2000 Ultimate Edition DVD. It adds in a moment where the T-1000 searches John's bedroom using its hypersensitive fingertips, and brings back the original ending for the film, which Cameron changed after negative responses at test screenings. It shows Sarah decades in the future, watching the adult John (now a senator) playing happily with his daughter. It was too drastic a change of tone, Cameron conceded, so he switched to the footage of the night-shrouded road that now ends the movie, though he kept the same moral-delivering voiceover.

wasn't like you couldn't have done this two years ago,' said Muren. 'It was more like you couldn't have done this a *week* ago. This movie pushed us right to the very edge.'

The results were jaw-dropping. The first time we see the T-1000 emerging from an exploded truck as a liquid-metal figure, fully animated but walking like a real human, it was, to quote *The Ringer* writer Alan Siegel, 'one of 20th century cinema's greatest "Holy shit!" moments.' But the effectiveness of the T-1000 went beyond groundbreaking VFX. Even a 2020s viewer might be surprised to learn that much of the character's visualization – nine of its 15 onscreen minutes, in fact – was achieved by Stan

Winston's team using prosthetics and puppetry. Like the foil-burst squibs for bullet impacts, for example, and the strange, twisted forms the T-1000 takes when blasted close-up, such as the 'Pretzel Man' concept, with its vortexed torso and dangling head, that we see during the climactic steel-mill showdown.

Then there was the actor who portrayed the inhuman infiltrator in its default form: that of a sleek street cop (once again revealing Cameron's anti-authoritarian streak). The 'Porsche' to Schwarzenegger's 'Panzer tank', as the director termed it. For the role, Cameron found another unknown, Robert Patrick, who had only previously done a few Roger Corman films. 'I think he was looking for somebody that looked like he could possibly just be a human, and yet could handle the intensity to be a Terminator,' said Patrick. This intensity manifested in surprising ways. When Patrick was required to sprint after Furlong on a motorcycle, he ran so fast that he actually caught up with the kid and tapped him on the shoulder. It might have been the first time anyone was asked to slow down on a James Cameron shoot.

Even by today's elevated standards, *Terminator 2* was a gargantuan production, delivering a string of escalating action set pieces – with a refreshingly low body count – that still impress. (More, in fact, than ILM's work on the T-1000, given the vast advances that have happened since in the CGI realm.) The final-act freeway chase is a particular highlight, not least when the T-1000's helicopter zooms *beneath* an underpass – a move that was not scripted, but was suggested to Cameron by stunt pilot Chuck Tamburro.

However, it was an incredibly exacting shoot on all the cast and crew, with the pressure of both time and expectation causing Cameron to volcanically vent in by now familiar ways. 'Everyone is kind of scared on set,' said Schwarzenegger. 'Because Jim doesn't use much psychology. He just screams at everybody. He just goes

off the deep end about any little thing.' When Hamilton's identical twin sister Leslie joined the shoot to step in as Sarah after the T-1000 mimics her near the film's end (Hamilton herself played the metal-imposter version), she made a point of telling Cameron not to yell at her. Otherwise, she warned him, they would both walk. Some of the crew wore T-shirts that read: '*Terminator 3*: Not With Me'. (These were not entirely original; '*Alien 3*: Not With Me' T-shirts had been worn by the *Aliens* crew five years earlier.)

Yet, as ever, every criticism of Cameron's workplace manner came with the admission that he always knew what the hell he was doing, and that his perfectionism would pay off. During one very difficult day, Patrick remembers Cameron reassuring him, 'Hey, look man, we're creating something. This is film history we're doing right now. It's never been done.'

He was not wrong. And the results spoke for themselves. The weekend the film was released, it accounted for more than half of all cinema tickets sold in the United States, making it the biggest-ever R-rated movie. It went on to gross more than $150 million worldwide, amply rewarding Carolco for all its unprecedented expense. In his review for the *Los Angeles Times*, Kenneth Turan described *Terminator 2* as 'one hell of a wild ride, a Twilight of the Gods that takes no prisoners and leaves audiences desperate for mercy.' *The Hollywood Reporter*'s critic, meanwhile, was so boggled by ILM and Winston's work that he closed his review by saying, 'We will forgo passing judgement on the special effects contributors. . .as their accomplishments are simply beyond our level of understanding.' Unsurprisingly, those effects won the movie one of its four Oscars at the Academy Awards, and paved the way for future ILM triumphs. 'If we hadn't

**LEFT:** Once again, playing a Terminator required Schwarzenegger to undergo hours of prosthetics application.

had *Terminator 2*,' reflected Muren, 'we wouldn't have been able to do *Jurassic Park*'. (Steven Spielberg's dinosaur-resurrecting hit was another groundbreaking triumph Muren shared with Winston two years later, which for a short time Cameron had hoped to direct himself.)

Even future Cameron, usually a harsh critic of his younger self's work, had something good to say about the film when interviewed for a 30th anniversary retrospective piece. 'I have been surprised at how well it holds up,' he said, before returning to one of his favourite themes. 'It's almost, in a funny way, more germane now than it was when it came out, because AI is now a real thing that we have to deal with, and then it was a fantasy like HAL 9000 [in *2001: A Space Odyssey*].' Perhaps as the result of being made in less troubling times, the film ends on an optimistic note, which its no-less apocalyptic sequels (none of which were directed by Cameron) ignored. Having apparently averted Judgment Day, Sarah Connor admits in a voiceover that she now faces the future 'for the first time, with a sense of hope. Because if a machine, a Terminator, can learn the value of human life, maybe we can too.'

After the film's success, Cameron must also have felt hope for his own future. Schwarzenegger had not been wrong: he

**ABOVE:** The first appearance of the T-1000 in full liquid-metal form was both a callback to *The Terminator* and an industry-changing visual effect, courtesy of ILM.

had made a movie that *anyone* would find hard to top. Except for Cameron himself, perhaps. Though, by concluding his tale of time-travelling robot hitmen, he had also ended a four-film run of big-scale sci-fi. It was time for a change of pace. To make a movie, for once, that only featured human characters. Something smaller, and more intimate, perhaps.

*'I married Rambo!'*

# TRUE LIES
## 1994

During Alfred Hitchcock's romantic caper *To Catch a Thief*, stars Cary Grant and Grace Kelly kiss and embrace as fireworks go off in the night sky behind them, suggesting the kind of hot, bright passion that the director was unable to depict more literally back in 1955. It was a scene James Cameron remembered well, and would riff on while making his eventual *Terminator 2* follow-up *True Lies*. Not that he usually goes in for homages. Aside from a brief reference to *The Third Man* in *Aliens* (where we see Newt's fingers reaching up through a grate), he rarely emulates other filmmakers. But he was determined to outdo Hitchcock's fireworks – in a way that few other filmmakers would dare.

Towards the end of *True Lies*, its heroic secret agent Harry Tasker (Arnold Schwarzenegger, in his first and last non-Terminator role for Cameron), has managed to rekindle his low-energy marriage to his office worker wife Helen (Jamie Lee Curtis) – who was previously unaware of his real vocation – by accidentally embroiling her in a mission to stop an Islamic terrorist cell in possession of rogue nukes. After a very narrow escape in the Florida Keys, where one of those warheads is timed to explode, Harry and Helen lock lips as the sky behind them flashes white and a mushroom cloud

**ABOVE:** Romance Cameron style: Harry and Helen Tasker (Arnold Schwarzenegger and Jamie Lee Curtis) rekindle their marriage as a rogue nuke detonates in the Florida Keys.

billows from its blast point. They are so blissfully wrapped up in each other, they do not even notice a nuclear detonation.

In his previous movies, Cameron had depicted nuclear explosions as moments of either extreme retribution or ultimate dread. Here, he set off The Bomb for the sake of a gag. Boom boom. 'Some people will find it inappropriate for a comedy,' he predicted. But, he added, 'I wanted to push some buttons with that scene.'

*True Lies* certainly did push buttons. Though not in ways that Cameron anticipated.

The two years between *Terminator 2*'s release and the start of production on *True Lies* were not exactly restful for Cameron. He managed to negotiate an impressive $500 million deal between Lightstorm and 20th Century Fox, whereby he could put any movie he liked into production – with complete creative control – as long as it did not cost more than $70 million. He also co-founded visual effects company Digital Domain with Stan Winston, which would become Hollywood's second biggest after ILM. Meanwhile, he went through his third divorce, with Kathryn Bigelow, before embarking on a relationship with his *Terminator* star Linda Hamilton.

All of which must have been on his mind when Arnold Schwarzenegger pitched him a new movie idea. The actor had recently watched *La Totale!*, a French farce directed by Claude Zidi, about a spy whose bored wife thinks he is just a dull office drone. After discovering she has embarked on an affair with a pick-up artist who coincidentally pretends to be a secret agent, he resolves to 'treat' her to a fake mission, before the real bad guys intervene and all is revealed. Schwarzenegger thought it had remake potential. Cameron agreed. 'I saw the film as an anti-James Bond, a reality check on the uber-male fantasy,' he said. He also discerned why it had connected with his friend, saying to Schwarzenegger, 'It's because you're a husband and a father and this is a way for you to process your reality…This is about giving that superhuman character that you play feet of clay, grounding him in a way where he can go out and do all this amazing stuff, but then he's got to come back and deal with his daughter and his wife.' Given his own demanding career and his trio of failed marriages, it is fair to say Cameron may have been projecting a little, here, too.

**RIGHT:** British actor Art Malik as terrorist leader Aziz, during the film's skyscraper-rooftop climax.

## Cameron on script: *Strange Days* (1995)

Cameron's never hidden the fact that he finds screenwriting difficult. This is why he tends to start any project with a long treatment (or 'scriptment') and ropes in friends to help. It is also why, he claimed, he preferred to write on the most uncomfortable chair he could find, so he would get the job done quicker to get out of it.

*Strange Days* was a script that ultimately defeated him. A high-tech film noir set on the last two days of 1999, it had been bouncing around in his head since the mid-1980s. All the main beats were there in his original five-page scriptment: the protagonist, Lennie Nero, as a black-market peddler of digitally captured sensory experiences (usually depicting sex or crime); the killing of a rap star by racist cops recorded on one of these 'clips'; the climax occurring during the biggest party of the millennium, in a Los Angeles so oppressively crime-ridden it is virtually a war zone. Nero fiddles while LA burns, then he achieves 11th-hour redemption as '2K' kicks off.

By 1992, when he was certain he would never have a chance to make *Strange Days* himself, Cameron pitched the film to Kathryn Bigelow (by now his ex-wife), who loved the concept and urged him to finish it. However, by the time he started on *True Lies*, the script was still incomplete, as he struggled with heavier dialogue and lighter action than he was used to. 'I wanted Elmore Leonard to come to me like Elvis came to Christian Slater in *True Romance* and tell me how to do this shit,' he said. When no such inspiration came, he held up his hands and hired Jay Cocks (one of Martin Scorsese's collaborators) to complete the screenplay – though Cameron would produce the film, too.

While the movie ultimately flopped, it was stylishly shot by Bigelow and still makes for interesting viewing today. Ralph Fiennes is counterintuitively impressive as the sleazy-but-charismatic Lennie, while the use of first-person POVs to depict some truly horrifying crimes (including a rape-murder) creates a troubling sense of viewer complicity. And despite its dystopian vibe, it actually ends on a touchingly hopeful note as Lennie finds true love amid all the confetti and ticker tape, with Angela Bassett's tough-but-moral security specialist Mace. As Cameron once claimed, all his films are basically love stories.

Around this time, he had actually been working on a serious, small-scale drama – an intended antidote to his exhausting run of blockbusters. Based on the real-life case of Billy Milligan, who had been acquitted as a serial rapist by pleading he suffered dissociative identity disorder, *The Crowded Room* was a script Cameron was co-writing with *The Abyss* actor Todd Graff, and he had John Cusack lined up for the lead role. However, a bitter disagreement over the rights forced Cameron to ditch the project.

With the demise of *The Crowded Room*, going serious lost its appeal, and Cameron instead embraced the new challenge of tackling humorous material. 'In some ways *True Lies* is one of the scariest movies I've done,' he said, 'because tonally it was a comedy.' His previous films all contained comedic elements, from the Terminator's selection of 'Fuck you, asshole' in its 'TermoVision' menu of dialogue options, to the oil workers' banter in *The Abyss*. But this was 'a French farce writ large', and required him to flex different muscles. He even sought the input of a team of comedy writers, before rejecting all but one of their suggested jokes. The sole survivor was the climactic zinger Schwarzenegger delivers when he launches an air-to-air missile with lead terrorist Aziz (British actor Art Malik) dangling from it: 'You're fired.'

As the inherently explosive nature of this gag suggests, going small-scale also lost its appeal to Cameron during the process of adapting *La Totale!* 'I just took the bones of that story and blew it up to a massive scale,' he said. 'Big action set pieces and helicopters and jets and flamethrowers and all that sort of thing. . .'

Cameron did not just go big in relation to the French original. He went big in relation to, well, everything. Principal photography began in August 1993 with a sequence that saw Harry taking on a trio of terrorists in a public toilet. It was supposed to take a day of filming, but on the day Cameron decided to upscale the shoot-out

**ABOVE:** Schwarzenegger in the public toilet shoot-out scene, which ended up taking a week to film.

and ordered production designer Peter Lamont (the Bond veteran who had worked with him on *Aliens*) to make the set three times bigger. In the end it took the best part of a week. Unsurprisingly, by the close of production – which massively overran – *True Lies* had bulked up far beyond the $70 million limit of Cameron's Fox deal. In fact, it had surpassed *Terminator 2* as the biggest-ever movie, with an estimated final budget of $120 million. 'I'm not afraid of taking a risk with an awful lot of money,' he said on release. 'The more successful *Terminator 2* was, the less it cost.'

There is no doubt that *True Lies* succeeds as an action spectacle. It exemplifies Cameron's ability to orchestrate mayhem and layer up kinetic sequences in impressive and unexpected ways. When Aziz jumps on a motorcycle in an early pursuit scene, for example, Harry gives chase on the back of a police horse, galloping through

**ABOVE:** A street-chase scene where Harry commandeers a police horse to pursue the motorcycle-riding Aziz.

city streets. Until, that is, the chase moves into a hotel, up a pair of grand glass elevators and onto the roof. At one point during the filming of this logistically tricky sequence, Schwarzenegger nearly fell foul of his mount. 'The horse freaked out and almost stepped off the roof,' he recalled. 'If it had taken one more step, we would have both fallen more than 30 feet to the ground.'

Later in the film, Harry is once again on Aziz's tail, except this time the villain has a couple of nuclear warheads and Helen held hostage in a limo, speeding along the Seven Mile Bridge in Florida, with Harry in a helicopter and a pair of Harrier jump jets as backup. The scene where they blow out a section of the bridge was achieved through a combination of utterly convincing model work with inventive use of a decommissioned stretch of the bridge, which had a section removed.

It is off the edge of this section that Helen's limo plummets, just as Harry grabs her, reaching from the skids of his chopper and plucking her from the car's sunroof. While the last-minute rescue itself was executed with a stunt performer (Donna Keegan), Curtis still had to perform the majority of the scene while hanging out of a remote-control limo going at 120 kmh, and even agreed to dangle from the helicopter to achieve one of the film's most memorable shots: a close-up of Helen shrieking as the ocean sweeps by below. Cameron himself was leaning out of the helicopter operating the camera, having decided that if Curtis was willing to do it, so should he. 'It was like he wouldn't let me take the risk without taking it right along with me,' said Curtis, who, for all the screaming, remembered the moment as 'magical'.

**ABOVE:** Jamie Lee Curtis took a very active role in the hugely impressive Seven Mile Bridge action sequence.

Yet this was not even the film's climax. That involves Harry commandeering one of the jets to rescue his 14-year-old daughter Dana (Eliza Dushku) from Aziz and his gang, who have hunkered down at the top of an under-construction skyscraper. Not only did this sequence involve a real building, complete with a construction crane, it also necessitated creating a life-size model of the Harrier, cast in fibreglass from one of the real planes, on which the stunt performers would clamber and dangle 90 metres above the streets of Miami.

For most of the scenes, Cameron had visual effects supervisor John Bruno of Digital Domain (making its debut with *True Lies*) mount the 14-metre-long jet model on a multi-axis motion base to tilt and tip it on the skyscraper's roof. This enabled Schwarzenegger, Malik and Dushku to be shot against real Miami backgrounds far below, rather than green screens. 'The first time I saw that, my jaw dropped,' said Curtis. 'It's outrageous what he did. And it went flawlessly.'

Though it was tough on the actors. Schwarzenegger recalled Cameron banning toilet breaks during the shoot, which made his cockpit-based scenes especially taxing. 'I am suspended 20, 30 stories up in the air and I have to go to the bathroom,' the star said. 'Jim screams at me, "No, you can't, you're now a military man on a mission!" Cameron would rather pee in his pants than leave the scene when things are clicking along.'

Once again, stories about the director's tyranny radiated from the set. He took to barking orders like a general, his voice amplified by a huge bank of speakers, giving him the nickname Mr Microphone. 'People who would screw up constantly would hear about it in a very direct manner,' said Tom Arnold, the sitcom star cast as Harry's crass sidekick Gib. Yet, as ever, those stories were accompanied by reports of Cameron's strokes of genius. When the rooftop scenes were done and the crew started lowering the Harrier model using the construction crane, the director saw and seized an opportunity to actually dangle the model 30 stories above the street, and use a helicopter to film the stunt performers atop it. This created some of the film's most astonishing shots without the need for extensive VFX.

Few reviews of *True Lies*, when it was finally released in July 1994, failed to applaud its high-end spectacle. 'James Cameron is a master of action,' wrote critic Roger Ebert, 'and when he's doing his thing, no one does it better. . .On the basis of stunts, special effects and pure action, it delivers sensationally.' However, like many critics, Ebert also provided a caveat. Between its opening and closing stunt-packed salvos, the film presents a quieter middle act in which Harry suspects Helen of infidelity with the slimy fake-spy Simon (played by Bill Paxton). Despite all his own deceptions and flirtations, a fuming Harry diverts his agency's resources to expose and potentially punish them. After anonymously interrogating Helen in a brutally intimidating manner and satisfying himself of her innocence, he decides to then use those resources to give her the thrill she seeks with a fake assignment. This involves compelling Helen to pose as a prostitute and perform a striptease for a shadowy

**ABOVE:** Tia Carrere as the villainous art dealer Juno Skinner, who allies with 'The Crimson Jihad' terrorists.

villain (actually Harry himself, operating an audio-tape player that delivers his instructions in a sleazy French accent). As Ebert notes, 'If you take a step back from the movie and really think about the trick the spy is playing on his wife, it's cruel and not funny.'

He was hardly alone in noticing this. In fact, other commentators took outright offence. Despite ending the film as Harry's consensual partner in espionage, there is absolutely nothing empowering about Helen's journey, believed *Los Angeles Times* writer Carol Treadwell. She 'is a woman defined by what she can't do to defend herself (anything), what she can't figure out (anything) and who will figure it out for her (her husband). She is a desperate and ineffectual figure. . .marked for humiliation.' Aside from these 'grossly sexist dynamics', Treadwell also highlighted one of the film's most distasteful jokes, delivered by Tom Arnold: 'Women. . .can't live with 'em, can't kill 'em.'

It is no less difficult to ignore the disturbing treatment of Helen (never satisfactorily addressed by Cameron, who brushed the criticism off by saying that not every scene in a film needs to be 'politically correct') than its questionable depiction of Arabs. Aziz aside, the terrorists of 'The Crimson Jihad' are, for the most part, depicted as cartoonish and bumbling when they are not delivering cowardly death-squeals as Harry guns them down. The body counts of Cameron's last two films were relatively low (not counting Sarah Connor's nuclear dream in *Terminator 2*), but now he allowed dozens to die: all with brown skin.

Boycotts of the film were called for by the National Council on Islamic Affairs and the American Arab Relations Committee, with members of various Arab American groups picketing its release in many cities in the United States. Rather ineffectively, 20th Century Fox had tried to mollify early complaints by adding an 11th-hour disclaimer to the credits which reads, 'This film is a work of fiction and does not represent the action or beliefs of a particular culture or religion.'

Similar to the accusations of misogyny, Cameron shrugged it all off. With the collapse of the Soviet Union, he had just cast around for 'some convenient villains', he said. 'It could [have been] anybody. I could have picked Irish terrorists.'

Cameron's apparently random choice would become uncomfortably prescient with the atrocity of 9/11 seven years later. And it was this, rather than the criticisms of *True Lies,* that put him off making a sequel. 'Terrorism is no longer something to take as lightly as we did in the first one,' he said in early 2003. 'I just can't see it happening given the current world climate.' Eventually, in 2010, he was happy enough with that climate to put a TV-series remake into development, though its eventual arrival in 2023 as a CBS show starring Steve Howey and Ginger Gonzaga was poorly reviewed and cancelled after one season. But back in 1994, even immediately after *True Lies'* $379 million success at the box office, Cameron was preparing to dive deep into a very different project.

**BELOW:** The controversial striptease scene, which Curtis choreographed herself.

‘I’m the king of the world!’

# TITANIC
1997

When the world's most powerful media baron and the director of Hollywood's most expensive movie ran into each other during the summer of 1996, it was not a comfortable encounter. After all, that movie – James Cameron's *Titanic*, now deep in post-production – was being funded, for the most part, by that mogul – namely Rupert Murdoch, chairman and CEO of News Corporation, which owned the studio 20th Century Fox. By this time, *Titanic* had achieved worldwide notoriety as an out-of-control production that had been beset by mishaps, run over schedule and gone hugely over budget, to a cost of $200 million. Its July release date had just been pushed back to 19 December. To make matters worse, Fox's other big summer movie *Speed 2: Cruise Control* had just sunk at the box office. So, when Cameron bumped into Murdoch in one of

**BELOW:** For *Titanic*'s modern-day segments, Cameron cast Golden Age star Gloria Stuart as the 100-year-old Rose.

the studio's corridors, after yet another fraught meeting with the Fox suits, the tension was palpable.

'I guess I'm not your favourite person,' said Cameron. 'But the movie is going to be good.'

Murdoch eyed the 43-year-old director coldly. 'It had better be a bit better than good,' he growled.

Cameron didn't really need to be told this. Back at his edit suite, where he was wrestling with 12 days' worth of footage and an unprecedented 500 visual effects shots, he had an even harsher reminder of the necessity of success. Taped up next to his screen was a razor blade, with a note-to-self: 'Use in case film sucks'.

It was gallows humour, of course, but says much about Cameron's state of mind during the most precarious moment of

**BELOW:** Billy Zane on top cad form as Cal Hockley, fiancé to the 17-year-old Rose (Kate Winslet).

his career. As he later reflected, 'When we were in the thick of it on that film, we just assumed we were doomed and we'd never work again.' However, the fate of *Titanic* would be the very inverse of its subject. In April 1912, the supposedly unsinkable pinnacle of Edwardian engineering ended up on the Atlantic's floor. But Cameron's supposedly ill-fated movie about that tragedy ended up being the most successful film in history.

Just as nobody was more aware of the pressure on *Titanic* than Cameron, nobody better appreciated just how unlikely it was that the guy behind a string of high-octane, pyrotechnic sci-fi/action blockbusters should get behind the helm of a costume-drama romance, which he had originally pitched to Fox boss Peter Chernin as '*Romeo and Juliet* on a boat'. Indeed, Cameron liked to joke about that pitch meeting, which happened in March 1995. 'So, I go in and I say, "Okay guys, here's the picture: takes place in 1912. It's a period drama. We can't have any stars because the characters are too young. And it's probably going to cost north of $100 million. And everybody dies at the end and there's no sequel possibilities. What do you think? Sound good!?"'

Fortunately, there was enough trust in Cameron for Chernin to tentatively commit. Some of cinema's biggest successes had been intimate romances set against huge historical events, like *Gone With the Wind* and *Doctor Zhivago.* And there was clearly potential for big-screen spectacle here – Cameron's speciality. Plus, the director had an interesting angle: he wanted to frame the story with a modern-day section that would involve treasure-seekers exploring the wreck, and he had already lined up Russian science vessel *Akademik Mstislav Keldysh,* its crew, and its two high-tech Mir submersibles – each carrying a 35mm camera adapted for deep-sea usage by his brother Mike – to film the real ship on the ocean bed.

**ABOVE:** Bill Paxton made his fourth appearance in a Cameron film as modern-day treasure hunter Brock Lovett.

It was as a 'gearhead' that Cameron was first drawn to RMS *Titanic*. In 1987, he had watched Dr Robert Ballard's National Geographic documentary about the wreck, and been impressed by Ballard's use of ROVs (remotely operated vehicles). Seeing robots in the deep ocean was, he said, 'a science-fiction dream come true. Inner-space exploration with all the trappings of outer-space

**ABOVE:** Leonardo Dicaprio and Kate Winslet became close friends during the long and difficult shoot for *Titanic*.

fiction.' Those images of the liner stayed with Cameron until, in 1992, he re-watched Roy Ward Baker's *A Night to Remember* (1958) and decided it was time for a fresh take on the event. One that, with the advantage of modern effects, would give the audience a more direct and emotionally intense experience of how it must have felt to be on that iceberg-stricken ship as the Atlantic gulped it down.

The idea of foregrounding a romance between two young lovers came during Cameron's historical research. He was struck by the social divisions that marked the tragedy, especially the statistic that women in First Class had a 97 per cent chance of survival, while men in Third Class had only a 16 per cent chance. You could not get more star-crossed than a romance between an upper-class girl and a boy from steerage on a ship only 96 hours away from destruction. They needed to be young enough for one of them – the girl, Rose – to feasibly still be alive in the modern-day segments. And their youthfulness, Cameron figured, would just heighten the emotionality: 'There is no purer, more consuming love than first love.' But presenting that love convincingly was, he said, the toughest artistic challenge of making the film. 'Boy meets girl is the oldest story ever told, so how do you make that interesting and exciting and new?'

The key to getting it right was in the chemistry of the actors he would cast, and much of *Titanic*'s ultimate success can be attributed to the fact that, in this sense, Cameron absolutely nailed it. He had been initially resistant to casting director Mali Finn's recommendation of 20-year-old Kate Winslet for the role of Rose DeWitt Bukater, the upper-class 17-year-old who is being railroaded into a loveless marriage with an utter cad (played by Billy Zane) when fresh-faced drifter Jack Dawson interrupts her during a poop-deck suicide attempt. The British actor had made her debut just over a year earlier in Peter Jackson's *Heavenly Creatures*, and had further proven herself as a strong and daring performer in Ang Lee's *Sense and Sensibility*. The problem for Cameron was that these were both period dramas, and he wanted his actors to have some contemporary edge. However, Winslet impressed him in her audition and then won him over by phoning him and almost demanding that he cast her. 'She was so positive and aggressive,' he said. He saw in her the kind of girl who would dive into icy water with an axe to rescue her manacled beau, if needs be.

The role of Jack, meanwhile, required a young actor with enough maturity to embody the character's worldly-wise vagabond spirit. Cameron cited novelist Jack London as an influence, but it's not hard to detect the director himself in there, too, given Jack's self-confident resourcefulness and artistic proclivity (all his art is in fact drawn by Cameron, including the plot-crucial nude of Rose). Jack even makes a reference to growing up in Chippewa Falls, Wisconsin, which of course shares its name (if not the spelling) with Cameron's own hometown of Chippawa Falls. So, it should not have been surprising that the tall, blond Cameron should cast the tall, blond Leonardo DiCaprio – then 21 years old and already the recipient of a Best Supporting Actor Oscar nomination for his portrayal of a developmentally disabled boy in 1993's *What's Eating Gilbert Grape?*

Although, initially, DiCaprio thought the role beneath him: too clean-cut and lacking in the kind of darker shading that he found interesting. This time it was Cameron who had to do the convincing, eventually winning over the young star by explaining why this would be a unique challenge. 'When you don't have a [character with] a drug addiction, or a physical or mental affliction – these overt actions, almost props – you have to rely on something more inward and subtle,' he told DiCaprio. 'To be charming and charismatic every moment on the screen is a much bigger challenge. It's the thing Jimmy Stewart did when 10,000 [others] couldn't.'

In early screen-chemistry tests, Cameron saw Winslet and DiCaprio clicking perfectly, and, sure enough, they'd win audiences over, too. Many were teenage DiCaprio fans, who'd return to see the film multiple times, contributing significantly to its colossal, record-smashing $1.8 billion box office. Tellingly, the biggest

**LEFT:** DiCaprio as vagabond artist Jack Dawson, based partly on writer Jack London, and partly on Cameron himself.

weekend of its initial theatrical run was Valentine's Day weekend 1998, two months after it released. Winslet and DiCaprio, meanwhile, became the best of friends during the production. 'We were partners,' recalled DiCaprio. 'We'd unload the stresses of the shoot to each other, vent to each other, and watch out for each other.' There was certainly a multiplicity of stresses to unload: the long night shoots, the effort and discomfort of shooting in water, the sheer overwhelming scale of it all. Because as far as movie shoots went, *Titanic* was an endeavour truly like no other.

That endeavour began many months before the film even officially started production, under literally high-pressure circumstances. During the autumn of 1995, Cameron, with a select film crew and the Russian submariners of the *Keldysh*, made 12 dives to the *Titanic's* wreck, 3,650 metres below the surface of the Atlantic and about 650 kilometres from the coast of Newfoundland, to shoot it in greater cinematic detail than had ever been achieved. It was a fraught and patience-testing process, yielding only 12 minutes of footage for each 10-hour trip.

It was dangerous, too. The Russians referred to Cameron's bespoke camera as 'the cannon', because if its casing cracked under pressure, the resulting implosion would blast its contents directly back at the Mir behind it at the speed of a cannonball. This fortunately never happened, though there was a close shave when an unusually strong current swept up Cameron's submersible and tossed it around, leading to the rapid depletion of its battery and its power cutting out. After dropping ballast, it took three attempts to break free of the current and return to the surface in freezing-cold darkness, a gruelling ascent that took five hours.

But the results were worth such hair-raising adventures, the director felt. In his review of the film, *The New Yorker* critic Anthony Lane highlights the VFX sequence where Cameron transitions

## Unmade Cameron: *Spider-Man*

'The greatest movie I never made', said Cameron, was *Spider-Man*. During the early 1990s, even before *Terminator 2*, he was in talks to make it with Carolco, which had snapped up the rights to the popular Marvel Comics superhero. Cameron was arguably the ideal filmmaker to take on the first-ever cinematic adaptation of Stan Lee and Steve Ditko's webslinger, being both a fan of the source material since childhood and obviously more than capable of meeting all the incredible action and VFX demands the project would bring. Having written a scriptment in 1991, it looked like it might finally come together as his next movie after *True Lies*, rather than *Titanic*. Unfortunately, Carolco became embroiled in a complicated legal battle over the rights and went bankrupt (along with Marvel) in 1996. So, Cameron's plans, as he put it, 'ended up in limbo and I moved on to other things.'

His version would have been remarkably different to the one eventually made by Sam Raimi in 2002 after Sony Pictures extricated the rights. It was certainly pitched at an older audience, featuring Peter Parker saying 'motherfucker' and having sex with Mary-Jane Watson at the top of the Brooklyn Bridge. It also involved a villain based on the comic-book character of Electro, as well as an intended cameo from Arnold Schwarzenegger as Otto Octavius (aka Dr Octopus) for the sake of a sequel tease.

However, there was one Cameron-conceived element that survived in the Raimi version. After securing the blessing of Lee, he changed the teenaged hero's improbably home-made mechanical web shooters to biological ones. 'Why couldn't he have these little spinnerets in his wrist that only come out when he needs them?' reasoned Cameron, who saw in them 'a metaphor for puberty. . .with all the confusion and anxiety that happens when your body changes.' All of which is right there in the 2002 film, even though Cameron has no writing credit. 'That wasn't terribly polite of them,' he told his biographer Rebecca Keegan in 2009.

from the rusticle-gnawed husk of the real ship, explored in the story by Bill Paxton's Brock Lovett, to its heyday recreation by Digital Domain. 'As if in fulfilment of a wish, she *melts* into life,' Lane writes. 'This may be the most beautiful special effect ever seen. . .As bracing a prospect of rebirth as you could hope to imagine.'

As well as making Cameron a first-hand expert on the layout and look of the vessel, his expeditions had a crucial emotional effect, too. After his first dive, his jubilation at the achievement of landing on the *Titanic*'s deck was soon tempered by the realization that he had just toured the final resting place of 1,517 people. 'The enormity of the tragedy, the loss of life, the horror of what it must have been like hit me,' he said. 'I made a vow to myself at that moment to stop being an astronaut and to honour the place, and the event, by taking time on every dive to take the wreck in.'

That commitment powered Cameron's relentless perfectionism throughout the shoot proper. He never failed to remind others of the tragedy's weight. Early in the schedule, while filming the scenes where passengers freeze to death in the ocean's icy waters, he gave the following speech to the floating performers: 'I want to be able to hear you scream, like you mean it.

**ABOVE:** Cameron and production designer Peter Lamont's recreation of RMS *Titanic* by was astonishingly accurate.

Fifteen hundred people are going to die tonight. That's the entire population of the town I grew up in.' Even at his eventual moment of triumph, when he accepted the Oscar for Best Film in March 1998 – *Titanic*'s 11th win that night – he kept the tragedy in mind, calling for an uncomfortable moment of silence in respect for the victims of the disaster.

Cameron's quest for visual fidelity, immersive impact and emotional heft was so ambitious, it took the backing of more than one studio to bring it to completion. Having rapidly built a whole three-stage studio from the ground up on Mexico's Pacific coast, complete with the world's biggest water tank (containing 17 million gallons of water) to hold Cameron and production designer Peter Lamont's almost life-size 235-metre-long model of the ship, Fox partnered up with rival studio Paramount Pictures to share the financial burden, in return for distributing the movie domestically.

As keyed in as he was to the vast macro challenges of staging the liner's nosedive into the sea – with 250 performers, including 100 stuntpeople, clinging to or tumbling down its tilted deck during the most intense and logistically demanding days – the director was also obsessed with the micro aspects. He insisted that every piece of crockery, furniture and set decoration was accurate. And his across-the-board hands-on nature and granular attention to detail once again led to the firing of a cinematographer. Cameron's original choice, Caleb Deschanel, disagreed with the director over the look of the film (Cameron wanted it in full living colour; Deschanel envisioned what he felt a more period-appropriate limited palette), so was replaced with *True Lies*' Russell Carpenter only a few weeks into shooting.

As the production's unprecedented demands caused delays and pushed it behind schedule, and as the costs mounted, the unbearable pressure began to tell. Cameron's trademark sarcasm and his occasional bursts of rage led to some tense moments on set, with Winslet telling the *Los Angeles Times* that 'there were times I was genuinely frightened of him. He has a temper like you wouldn't believe.' Although, he never exploded at the actors, she

**RIGHT:** Rose wearing the film's diamond MacGuffin, the 'Heart of the Ocean'.

pointed out. 'He couldn't shout at us the way he did to his crew because our performances would be no good.'

Even the head of Fox Filmed Entertainment, Bill Mechanic, found himself at the receiving end of a Cameron eruption. After the studio boss visited Baja Studios to request some cost-saving cuts, the director shouted at him, 'If you want to cut my film you'll have to fire me, and to fire me you'll have to *kill* me! If you're such a fucking expert, then you can finish the movie yourself!' Of course, nobody was capable of stepping in and taking over the movie, least of all Mechanic. Cameron kept his job and would, in the end, accept a number of suggested cuts – even an entire

## Cameron on TV: *Dark Angel* (2000–2002)

Despite having a relatively short filmography which features a number of sequels, Cameron was never short of original ideas. One of his favourites in the late '90s was 'experimental girl': a young, genetically enhanced woman who lives in a not-too-distant future that suffers a kind of new dark age after all computing and communications are destroyed in a terrorist attack. Eventually, he decided it could work well as a TV show, and together with writer Charles Eglee (who had scripted *Piranha II*) devised *Dark Angel* for Fox TV, with Cameron himself directing the pilot. Characteristically, it had a big budget, bringing the first season in at around $10 million.

The show's most notable element was the casting of its main character, Max Guevara, providing Jessica Alba (then 19) with her screen debut. But despite its success, drawing an audience of 17 million, and largely positive reviews, Fox lost faith in it and shunted the show to a late Friday night slot for its second season, before cancelling it, against Cameron's expectation. 'So that was my 10-minute adventure into network TV land,' he said, describing the experience as 'despicable'.

waterlogged shoot-out sequence that cost $1 million, after test audiences responded badly to it.

In retrospect, he accepted that he could be a demanding and sometimes difficult person, and was sympathetic to Winslet, especially after she insisted her comments were taken out of context. But one thing he could not abide were the claims made in many reports during production that his set was dangerous, and that he mercilessly put people in harm's way. '*Titanic* got grim because it was hard work,' he admitted. 'It was physically taxing – the water and the sinking ship and all that.' But he was so insistent on defending his safety record that he wrote to the *Los Angeles Times* in response to a feature it ran on 19 April 1997 titled 'Epic-Size Troubles on *Titanic*'. 'Am I driven? Yes. Absolutely,' he said. 'Out of control? Never. Unsafe? Not on my watch.' His safety record on all his films, he stated, 'has been far above the industry norm. . .After 12 years of directing mammoth action sequences, I had one set injury requiring emergency treatment before *Titanic* (for a burn on the arm during *True Lies*)'. He then addressed the injuries that *did* occur, during *Titanic*'s spectacular poop-deck tilt sequence, in which three stunt players suffered broken bones as they piled up on the padded studio floor. 'This happened although the stunts were rigged according to industry standards and had been choreographed and rehearsed on video, on the set, for literally weeks in advance. Some might consider these injuries the "normal" hazards of stunt work. I do not. I elected to stop shooting the scene this way and instead incurred additional expense using computer animation to get the same result.' (In so doing, Cameron and Digital Domain set a new standard for convincingly representing normal human figures using CGI.)

One of the shoot's stranger mishaps occurred early in the production, while Cameron was shooting the modern-day scenes in Halifax, Nova Scotia. He and around 75 of the cast and crew began feeling unwell after their meal break, during which they'd eaten the mussel chowder. Fearing food poisoning, Cameron immediately forced himself to vomit, but even so, he began feeling oddly disorientated, his eyes turning blood red. He and the others affected were rushed to hospital, by which point people were hallucinating and freaking out – or embracing the unexpected high and partying in a hospital hallway conga line. After a toxicology test, it transpired that the chowder was heavily laced with PCP, a dissociative anaesthetic street drug. To this day, it remains a mystery as to who was responsible, though Cameron's unproven theory was that a fired crew member had spiked the soup after a disagreement with the on-set caterer.

Another charge levelled at Cameron by the press during the darkest days of his *Titanic* experience was that of profligacy; that it was unconscionable a film should cost so much, and he was irresponsible for letting the expenses mount up. However, as Cameron repeatedly pointed out, his sense of responsibility extended to giving up his percentage of the film's potential revenue. 'I did it,' he wrote in the *Los Angeles Times*, 'because I love this film.' One of the main reasons for it costing so much, he maintained, was the fact that its production had involved simultaneously building a new studio facility and one of history's biggest, most complex sets. Yet, he pointed out, the film wouldn't need to make much more than *True Lies* had to break even.

After publicly defending himself in a newspaper, Cameron decided the best way to deal with the media furore over his production would be to let it blow out – something the five-month release-date delay would certainly help with. 'They'll go right past us and fall on their face,' he told Fox boss Chernin. 'And then how are they going to resurrect the negative story five months later?' He wasn't wrong. By the time *Titanic* finally launched, word had leaked

**ABOVE:** Jack takes Rose 'flying' in one of the film's most celebrated moments.

from test screenings that it was actually very good, with confirmation provided by the reviews that landed following its world premiere at Shibuya's Orchard Hall theatre during the Tokyo Film Festival on 1 November 1997 – where Cameron and his now-wife Linda Hamilton were almost crushed by a 3,000-strong crowd of DiCaprio fans. *The Hollywood Reporter* declared the film 'a masterwork of big-canvas storytelling, broad enough to entrance and entertain yet precise and delicate enough to educate and illuminate.' The *New York Times*' Janet Maslin, meanwhile, described

it as 'the first spectacle in decades that honestly invites comparison to *Gone With the Wind.'*

This comparison would extend to *Titanic*'s box office. In the end, it did far more than break even, and, like *Gone With the Wind,* would become the highest-grossing movie yet made despite its three-and-a-quarter-hour running time necessarily limiting how often it could be screened each day. Buoyed by 'Leo-mania', it became a full-steam cultural phenomenon. And, while there is something to detractors' claims that Cameron's script clunks and grinds in places, his sheer emotional sincerity and devotion to telling a familiar story in an unexpectedly spectacular way outweighs any niggles. One might even forgive him for his cringey, Jack-quoting announcement at the Oscars that he was now 'King of the world!'

*Titanic* succeeded far beyond Cameron, or anyone's expectations. By applying his 'gearhead' blockbuster-crafting expertise to one of modern history's best-known and most resonant tragedies, he had created something universal. With the film's Oscars sweep including an Academy Award for directing, he had also graduated, in the eyes of the industry, from sci-fi-nerd bad boy to serious player.

**ABOVE:** While the water on set wasn't as cold as the Atlantic, shooting in it still proved gruelling for DiCaprio, Winslet and crew.

**PREVIOUS PAGE:** The almost life-size *Titanic* replica was one of the biggest and most complex sets ever created.

He made a fortune from the film, despite giving up his profit participation during production. More fundamentally, Cameron said, 'If you can make a movie that's basically a chick flick where everybody's wearing corsets and silly hats, and where everybody dies at the end and succeed, it kinda gives you permission to do anything.' *Titanic* was his 'get out of jail card,' he figured. 'I just took it as permission to go have fun.'

*'You might see something that nobody's ever seen before'*

# DEEP-SEA ADVENTURES
## 2002–05

**A** movie director taking a long hiatus is not unheard of in Hollywood. Terrence Malick withdrew from the industry for almost two decades, from 1978's *Days of Heaven* to 1998's *The Thin Red Line*, while Stanley Kubrick took an extensive sabbatical between *Full Metal Jacket* in 1987 and *Eyes Wide Shut* in 1999. So, the fact that James Cameron did not direct a single feature film between *Titanic* and the start of production on *Avatar* in 2006 is not in itself hugely remarkable.

Of course, given he had just had the biggest triumph of his career, it did seem a little odd he was not sticking around to capitalize on it. But he had also just had the toughest overall production experience of his career, so you might have forgiven any filmmaker for calling it a day, especially if it meant bowing out on a presumably unbeatable high. (Cameron apparently underlined this by quitting Digital Domain – with co-founder Stan Winston – after the company's board raised some post-*Titanic* conflict-of-interest concerns over his position as both CEO and a filmmaker client.) But this was 'Iron Jim', as *Premiere* magazine once dubbed him. Calling it a day was the last thing on his mind.

What makes Cameron's hiatus so remarkable is what he spent it doing: exploring some of planet Earth's most extreme environments. He joked at the time that he was 'the world's busiest unemployed filmmaker'. But the word 'busy' does not even begin to cover it. As Cameron later summed up: 'I spent eight years doing expeditions, building robots, building underwater cameras, building submersibles.' And, to help fund all this, he made a few documentaries along the way, too.

Cameron's urge to explore and discover is rooted in his childhood. 'I was surrounded by woods,' he said. 'I'd be out there catching frogs and snakes. [My parents] got me a microscope when I was 10 years old, and I started looking at pond water and seeing all the

**ABOVE:** French marine conservationist and oceanographer
Jacques Cousteau in 1984.

little micro-organisms that lived there. To me, it was just endlessly
fascinating, the natural world. They say exploration is just curiosity
acted upon. It's that need to see what's there beyond the edge of
your lights, to see the unknown for yourself.'

At first, his heart was set on outer space. But once he was old
enough to understand that visiting other planets was not likely
to happen, he focused instead on 'inner space'. One of his biggest
inspirations was Jacques Cousteau, the French oceanographer
and filmmaker, whose 1960s TV series *The Undersea World of
Jacques Cousteau* was essential viewing for the young Jim. The
undersea imagery that Cousteau shared, said Cameron, 'made
me realize that there are alien worlds right here on Earth that you
can explore for the cost of the scuba equipment'. So, at the age
of 16, he started taking lessons in this relatively new activity,

which had been co-invented by Cousteau around 20 years earlier. These lessons were taught in a swimming pool by ex-Navy guys at the YMCA in Buffalo, New York, around 40 km away from Cameron's home. They included harassment drills, which involved the instructor ripping off Cameron's mask, cutting off his air, and seeing how he coped. 'If you couldn't deal with it, you failed,' he said.

Over the following decades, as he ascended as a filmmaker and came to focus his creative energy on the *Titanic*, his urge to explore deeper into the ocean grew greater than his desire to make movies. Those dozen dives to the wreck in 1995 sparked something. He and his brother Mike had developed new technology to shoot the *Titanic* more effectively than ever before. 'That led naturally to creating new technology to go to places that people had never been before.'

First, he had unfinished business with a certain White Star Liner. Even after making *Titanic*, Cameron wanted to return to the wreck with improved equipment, including 3D cameras (which had so impressed him while making *T2-3D*) and Mike's slicker, smaller, cable-free ROVs – named Jake and Elwood, after the Blues Brothers. These were able to slip into areas of the ship that were previously unseen, including 'The Unsinkable' Molly Brown's state room, better preserved than anyone had expected, and filmed by Cameron with startling clarity.

With his friends Bill Paxton (aka *Titanic*-raider Brock Lovett) and Lewis Abernathy (who also appeared in the film as Brock's gauche buddy Lewis Bodine), as well as the Russian Mir veterans of the *Keldysh*, Cameron documented several more dives in September 2001, which he would combine with CG-assisted recreations to conjure up the ship's passengers for an IMAX audience in the Disney-released *Ghosts of the Abyss*.

## When Cameron met Soderbergh: *Solaris* (2002)

As early 2000s Hollywood collaborations go, it was surely one of the least likely: blockbuster-master Cameron teaming up with American-indie hero Steven Soderbergh, who had broken through in 1989 with *sex, lies, and videotape*. While Soderbergh had recently hit the mainstream with Oscar-winning war-on-drugs drama *Traffic* and the hugely popular *Ocean's 11*, his idiosyncratic, experimental style marked him out as a very different creature to Cameron, a child of the drive-in. Yet the two were united by a shared appreciation of Stanislaw Lem's 1961 psychological science-fiction novel *Solaris* and its 1972 adaptation by Soviet filmmaker Andrei Tarkovsky. Set on board a space station orbiting a strange planet, both film and book involve a visiting psychologist dealing with a phenomenon, caused by the world below, which apparently resurrects dead loved ones, including the psychologist's own wife.

Cameron had secured the rights to the book via Lightstorm Entertainment, with the intention of one day making his own adaptation, but never found the time to commit to it. He was happy to hand it over to Soderbergh when the director approached him and pitched his own take, which was less concerned with visual set pieces than Cameron had been, and more focused on the characters and relationships. In short, Cameron realized the material better played to Soderbergh's strengths than his own. (Although the novel's concept of a world being an immense life form would be echoed in *Avatar's* macro-ecological Eywa concept.)

It was a harmonious collaboration, but sadly the film – which starred George Clooney and Natascha McElhone – bombed at the box office, grossing only $30 million worldwide against a $47 million budget.

**ABOVE:** The rusting bow of RMS *Titanic*, as filmed by Cameron for 2003's *Ghosts of the Abyss*.

**ABOVE RIGHT:** Cameron's nimble ROVs were able to reach areas of the *Titanic* previously never seen on camera.

Paxton is the film's narrator and presenter, and is endearingly nervy during his first descent in a Mir, constantly asking his pilot questions about the oxygen gauge; as Cameron wryly noted, 'there's a real consistency in his character from *Aliens* through to this'. The director himself, in contrast with all those reports of his abrasive and Vesuvian behaviour on previous shoots, seems contented and relaxed throughout, even when things go wrong.

During one remote expedition through the ship's corridors, for example, Elwood loses power. Cameron risks his one remaining ROV to go rescue its 'brother', by towing it out. During this delicate operation, Jake becomes stuck. 'I don't know what to do,' says Cameron on camera, crestfallen rather than frustrated. Of course, within minutes he figures it out; after a little backtracking and a sharp push forwards, both ROVs are freed.

But he and his crew's jubilation was soon quelled when they returned to the surface. The date of the rescue was 11 September 2001, and within moments of climbing out of their subs, they were told about the terrorist attack on the World Trade Center: an event that paused, rather than cancelled, the remainder of filming at the *Titanic*, despite making their efforts seem 'trivial'. The finished film was released in 2003, but by this time Cameron had already sought out a very different shipwreck.

The DKM *Bismarck* was, on its launch by Nazi Germany in February 1939, one of the world's largest warships. After eight days terrorizing Allied shipping in the Atlantic during May 1941, she was sunk during a fierce battle with the Royal Navy. However, there was a debate over whether the *Bismarck* went down as the result of battle damage, or if it was because the Germans scuttled her. In 2002, Cameron decided to solve the mystery.

This required him to dive around 900 metres deeper than he had to the *Titanic*, given the *Bismarck*'s harder-to-access North Atlantic location (discovered, like *Titanic*, by Robert Ballard, in 1989). At this depth, said Cameron, 'we were certainly at the limit of our equipment'. The results were presented in a Discovery Channel documentary that aired on 8 December 2002, co-directed by Cameron with Gary Johnstone, and narrated by Lance Henriksen. As in *Ghosts of the Abyss*, footage of wreckage – this time swastika-adorned, and martially utilitarian rather than opulent – is combined with digital reconstructions of historical events, as well as details on the expedition itself, and the poignant presence of two of only three survivors of the sinking.

Using their nimble ROVs, the Cameron brothers were able to confirm the reason for the sinking, they believed. The worst of the

**TOP RIGHT:** Cameron with Bill Paxton, who in *Ghosts of the Abyss* gets to dive to the *Titanic* for real.

**BOTTOM RIGHT:** One of Mike and James Cameron's ROVs heads out from a wreck-visiting Mir submersible in *Ghosts of the Abyss*.

damage to the hull, it appeared, occurred when the ship crashed into the ocean floor, while the impact of the British torpedoes was surprisingly minimal. Even so, the documentary concludes that the ship would still have eventually sunk even if the Germans had not scuttled it.

When he originally decided to step away from feature filmmaking, Cameron had expected to return in two or three years. But he was enjoying himself far too much. The lure of the ocean's depths was far greater than that of Hollywood. 'We had a lot of fun,' he said in 2003. 'Feature films tend not to be as fun because there is no kind of underlying experience other than the making of the film itself. Whereas we were doing something really

**BELOW:** Cameron takes a dive in a new, self-designed submersible in 2005's *Aliens of the Deep*.

cool. For the first time in my life, I was working in a theatre of operations where the filming was secondary, which is an interesting concept.'

The stakes were higher, too, in terms of the personal risk taken, while Cameron was also working with a very different breed of collaborator: engineers and scientists, rather than actors and film crews. Together, these factors gave him a valuable new professional perspective. 'In the entertainment business, we always put that first, like it's the most important thing in the world, and everything is all very self-referential within that reality bubble,' he said. 'But I've been in lots of environments where they don't even think about movies. We don't even exist for them!'

**BELOW:** A hydrothermal vent, as seen in *Aliens of the Deep*. The film brings life to an environment untouched by sunlight.

Cameron's enjoyment of working with non-showbiz people is most apparent in his 2005 documentary *Aliens of the Deep*, which was another 3D IMAX Disney production. For this, he brought together NASA scientists and marine experts to dive down to various hydrothermal vents as deep as 3,000 metres – now in more advanced submersibles of his and Mike's own design. Here, they would study the 'extremophile' creatures, thriving despite never seeing sunlight, and extrapolate the likelihood of there being life in the Solar System beyond Earth, such as on the ice-packed Jovian moon of Europa.

As in *Ghosts of the Abyss*, Cameron presents as a calm and capable team leader, rather than a furious tyrant. His notorious alter ego 'Mij' is nowhere in sight, and indeed would never return.

It must have helped that, by this time, he was more settled in his personal life. Cameron's marriage to Linda Hamilton had disintegrated in 1998, but almost two years later he married *Titanic* supporting actor Suzy Amis (aka Rose's granddaughter), whom he is still with today. But, more pertinently, the change of collaborators was also changing him, for the better. 'You learn to deal with people from a place of respect,' he said. 'Before you open your mouth, if there's an assumption that you respect that person, you're gonna deal with them differently.' Perhaps the fact that, in this working environment, he no longer felt he could do anybody else's job as well (if not better) than them gave him a healthy dose of humility. And, apparently, further fuelled his enthusiasm.

'I'm Jim Cameron and here's the deal,' he announces early in *Aliens of the Deep*. 'I love this stuff: exploration. Real honest-to-God deep-ocean exploration. This is way more exciting than any made-up Hollywood special effects.' Weirdly, later in the documentary (co-directed with Steven Quale), made-up Hollywood VFX take over as Cameron visualizes a rather cheesy first contact between a few of his real-life scientists with *Abyss*-like aliens. But, as he states, the

**ABOVE:** One of the many bizarre creatures found by Cameron and his team in *Aliens of the Deep*.

strongest moments are when he encounters the strange creatures of the deep, existing in an environment so hazardous, the explorers have to be careful not to melt the glass of their subs' windows by getting too close to the 'liquid fire' spurting from the vents.

These deep-dwelling life forms, shimmering with bioluminescence and looking like nothing imaginable only years earlier, would partly inspire Cameron's next movie – as would the repeated success of his high-pressure 3D camera tests. By the time *Aliens of the Deep* was released, he had finally committed to returning to mainstream filmmaking. But what he was doing next would be *really* challenging. 'I'm only interested in it if it's really hard. Like, impossible. Like, there's no way that you can do it, no way you could survive and you're doomed going in,' he laughed. '*That's* interesting.'

# AVATAR
## 2009

ABOVE: With blue skin, feline features and towering height, the Na'vi of *Avatar* could never have been convincingly realized without performance-capture technology.

**G**reat leaps forward often happen as a series of small steps. And in the case of *'Project 880'*, as James Cameron's producing partner Jon Landau had dubbed it, the most significant of those steps happened late in 2005.

With the help of ILM, Cameron had been working hard on a single scene from the long-brewing sci-fi movie he hoped would be his long-awaited *Titanic* follow-up. The scene depicted the first meeting between the two main characters: a 2.7-metre-tall blue, cat-like alien huntress named Zuleika (played by *Lost*'s Yunjin Kim) and human soldier Josh (Daniel Bess), who is paralyzed from the waist down and has had his consciousness uploaded into a vat-grown body of the same blue-skinned species, the Na'vi, to better operate in the toxic atmosphere of Zuleika's deadly jungle world, Pandora. She rescues him from a pack of vicious six-legged creatures called viperwolves, then respectfully prays over their bodies, before chastising this clumsy interloper. In time, of course, they will fall in love.

The scene had been assembled as a prototype to convince 20th Century Fox to fund the movie that was truly titled *Avatar* (after those vat-grown bodies). Despite running for only 37 seconds, it had taken four months to put together, having been shot in high-definition 3D in a bare Los Angeles studio using new 'virtual camera' technology Cameron was developing.

The actors had performed in dot-covered leotards, their every movement and facial expression (including eye movements) captured by infrared sensors mounted all over a shooting space known as 'The Volume', to drive the performance of their fully CG, photoreal onscreen counterparts, in the midst of an entirely digitally conjured alien-forest environment. It was 'a live-action, real-time, director-centric performance-capture process,' said Cameron. 'In other words, as the actors perform, I'm able to see in the monitor not only what they might look like as their CG character, but the CG environment we've created, and direct them accordingly.'

The Fox executives, including chairman Tom Rothman, were impressed. This was far more advanced and emotionally engaging than Robert Zemeckis' recent foray into motion-capture, *The Polar Express*, with its unfortunately dead-eyed characters. It was even a notch above Peter Jackson and Weta Digital's achievement with Gollum (Andy Serkis) in *The Lord of the Rings* trilogy, which had originally inspired Cameron to push forward with this project, having previously deemed it technically unfeasible.

There were concerns, of course. Would an audience connect sufficiently with long-necked, blue-skinned aliens? Should the studio commit so much to something that came entirely from Cameron's brain, rather than an established intellectual property? And, more importantly, if it took four months to create 37 seconds, how long and how expensive would the process be for a two-hour-plus movie made this way? Still, they nervously gave Cameron a green light.

Just before the director and Landau left, one of the suits shook his head and told the pair, 'I don't know if we're crazier for letting you do this, or if you're crazier for thinking you *can* do this.' The ever-confident Cameron was sure he could. He just did not let on that, even after nailing the prototype, he still was not sure exactly *how*. He was heading into uncharted filmmaking territory to pioneer something he hoped would fundamentally change the cinematic experience – a '21st-century *Jazz Singer*', to quote *Empire* magazine. As Cameron would later describe it, making *Avatar* was like 'jumping off a cliff and knitting a parachute on the way down.'

In 1992, while setting up Digital Domain, Cameron wrote a 'Digital Manifesto', in which he set out his hopes and plans for the future of visual effects. Among these he mentioned 'performance capture', which would enable an actor to play a

**ABOVE:** Just like its Na'vi characters, the lush world of Pandora was conjured up by Weta Digital's state-of-the-art visual effects.

character with no limits to its physical appearance, as their movements would be recorded by a 'data suit' and applied to the character created in the computer. By 2005, he had two feature ideas that would enable him to adopt, progress and perfect this technique. One was *Battle Angel*, an adaptation of Yukito Kishiro's manga *Battle Angel Alita*, an action-driven cyberpunk take on *Pinocchio*, with a full-body cyborg girl instead of a wooden boy (see page 188).

The other was *Avatar*, Cameron's own creation, which he originally outlined in 1996 in an 80-page treatment, with the hope that Digital Domain could develop the tech to make it possible. He had 'a great script' for *Battle Angel*, but *Avatar* won 'the horse race', he said in 2007, simply because it had a better scene with which he could test his virtual-camera process, and show off the 3D he had been developing via his documentaries (intended less to have objects poking out at the audience in gimmicky ways, and more as an immersive 'wrap-around experience').

This apparently glib reasoning belies the fact that *Avatar* was Cameron's most personal work to date. 'I wanted to make a film that could encompass all my interests,' he said. Its origins go back to the fantastical drawings he created as a child, 'doodling on the back of my math notes in high school.' Not to mention his concept art for *Xenogenesis*, which includes an image of a tall, blue-skinned woman standing in magenta grass: a human biologically adapted for life on an alien world. *Avatar* was inspired, he said, 'by every single science-fiction book I read as a kid,' as well as the 'manly jungle adventures' of writers like H Rider Haggard and Rudyard Kipling. The visual-effects requirements of the film were further down the same trajectory he had been on since *The Abyss* and *T2*, while his deep-sea dives encouraged the 3D and further inspired the story's creatures and environments, not least their striking bioluminescence. Plus, as Cameron pointed

**RIGHT:** Sam Worthington as Jake Sully, with his vat-grown avatar behind, waiting for its consciousness upload.

**BELOW:** Jake, in avatar-form, receives an up-close-and-personal hunting lesson from Na'vi princess Neytiri (Zoë Saldaña).

**ABOVE:** Michelle Rodriguez plays Captain Trudy Chacón, who sides with the Na'vi for the film's final battle.

**FOLLOWING PAGE:** Jake proves his worth to Neytiri's people by bonding with a banshee, or ikran, and taking to the skies.

out, the whole concept of using an avatar to explore an environment unsuited to humans connected to his own employment of ROVs to reach and record places previously impossible to access. 'I've already done it, in a sense, flying robots through the hallways of the *Titanic*,' he said.

Certain visual elements recall previous Cameron adventures: the AMP (Amplified Mobility Platform) Suits are souped-up

### Cameron's cut: *Avatar: Special Edition* and *Extended Cut*

With *Terminator 2*, it seemed that Cameron had put out his final Special Edition; he had no inclination, for example, to re-release *Titanic* with its removed shoot-out sequence restituted, even when the film went back into cinemas with a 3D version (though this did correct the starfield seen above the sinking ship). However, even though the original *Avatar* clocked in at 162 minutes, after its success the director was soon back to his old running-time-stretching ways.

First, he assembled the *Special Edition* for a 2010 theatrical re-release, which is nine minutes longer, more due to the extension of existing scenes – such as Jake and Neytiri's love-making and the thanator assault on Quaritch's AMP Suit – than adding significant new ones. Then, for the film's home entertainment release, Cameron also put together the *Extended Cut*, which added a further eight minutes, bringing the running time to 178 minutes. Much of this comes from the Earth-set prologue, which Cameron had originally jettisoned, providing a taste of Jake's rough life on his overcrowded and heavily urbanized home planet, with its heavy shades of *Blade Runner's* Los Angeles. We find him literally lying in the gutter when the men in suits arrive to tell him about the death of his twin brother, kicking off the plot that will send him to the stars.

versions of *Aliens'* power-loader, and the human invaders are once more run by an amoral company – on the planet to mine 'unobtanium', a precious resource needed back on a dying Earth – backed up by colonial marine-like military heft in the form of SecOps. Meanwhile, Pandora alpha-predator the thanator is clearly a more feline version of the Alien Queen.

But there is a lot of *Titanic* in *Avatar*, too, even beyond the similarity of the film's scores (both written by James Horner). Like Jack and Rose, Jake Sully (the character formerly known as Josh, now played by Australian newcomer Sam Worthington) and Neytiri (formerly Zuleika, now beautifully played by Zoë Saldaña)

## Cameron on script: *Alita: Battle Angel* (2019)

After Cameron was turned on to Yukito Kishiro's *Battle Angel Alita* by his friend, Mexican director Guillermo del Toro, in the late 1990s, he hinted in interviews that it would be his next project: once he was done with *Dark Angel*, then after he had finally finished with *Avatar*. It had everything he loved: a strong female lead, commentary on the perils of technology, and futuristic world-building. But in the end, amid all his aquatic excursions, environmental initiatives and Pandoran preoccupations, he never found the necessary headspace or time to direct the film himself. So, he handed the script (co-written with Laeta Kalogridis) and around 600 pages of world-building notes to his pal Robert Rodriguez, director of *Desperado, Sin City* and the 3D *Spy Kids* movies.

'Robert and I have been looking for a film to do together for years, so I was pumped when he said he wanted to do *Battle Angel*,' Cameron said in October 2015, comparing their collaboration to 'two kids building a go-kart' and praising Rodriguez's 'technical virtuosity and rebel style.' It is fair to say he saw in the Texan director a kindred spirit, and it proved 'a dream collaboration,' Cameron said.

*Alita: Battle Angel*, as it was ultimately called, used much of the same technology as *Avatar*, including performance and facial capture – primarily for the title character (played by Rosa Salazar), with her large, manga-style eyes and synthetic body – and Simulcam, with Weta Digital heading up the VFX. However, unlike *Avatar*, it mostly took place on traditional sets, recreating the junk-town setting of Iron City at Rodriguez's Troublemaker Studios in Austin, Texas, with a mostly live-action cast (including Christoph Waltz, Jennifer Connelly, Mahershala Ali and Jackie Earle Haley).

Its blend of CGI and live action is impressively seamless, with Alita certainly representing a step forward in photoreality from *Avatar*'s Na'vi, while Rodriguez gives its pugilistic action sequences some zip and swagger. But neither the director's style nor Cameron and Kalogridis' script lift it above a sense of cyberpunk business as usual and, after opening to lukewarm reviews, the film barely broke even with a worldwide take of $405 million. As a result, its heavily baited sequel has yet to materialize, though in 2022, Cameron revealed that he and Rodriguez have made a 'blood oath' that it will one day happen.

fall in love despite coming from vastly different backgrounds. Except this time, it is the woman who is acting as the social mentor, educating Jake (secretly on a reconnaissance mission for the grizzled SecOps Colonel Quaritch, played by Stephen Lang) about Na'vi culture.

Once the script was finally written in April 2006, it also came freighted with environmental and anti-colonial themes. Along with the human scientists on Pandora, who are overseen by Dr Grace Augustine (Sigourney Weaver, happily returning to the Cameron-verse in a non gun-toting role), Jake learns that the Na'vi exist in balanced symbiosis with their environment, which has a global consciousness they call Eywa. So, inspired by his love for Neytiri, he turns on his human bosses, goes native, and fights against their environmentally rapacious efforts.

These themes did not go unnoticed by the executives at 20th Century Fox, who were concerned about a huge, mainstream movie being so overtly political. 'Is there a way to cut down on the hippy tree-hugging stuff?' Cameron was asked. An 'environmental message', they told him, could cost them '50 per cent of our box office'. Even so, he did not waver. 'It's a legitimate concern,' he said, 'but that's why I wanted to make the film in the first place.' After *Titanic*, he did not *need* to make another movie. So it was important to him that what he *did* make was personal and had 'some thematic value'. But he would also ensure their bottom line was protected by packing it full of action, adventure and spectacle. 'So I threw everything I had at making it a great piece of entertainment.'

'Everything' in this instance would require $237 million of Fox's money (despite the film having no big stars to eat up the budget), over two years in production and post-production, and a record-breaking 1,000 terabytes of computing memory to render the film's 2,000 VFX shots (twice each, for 3D).

The *Avatar* shoot did not involve life-size models of sinking ships, Harrier jump jets, extensive underwater photography or hazardous location shooting. It was also notably free of directorial incandescence – aside from the occasional 'bark,' as Worthington put it; 'but only if you don't meet his standard.' Even so, its tribulations were no less intense than his previous projects, due to its inherently experimental nature. This required the development of new technology, which was often being tested live, and a need for constant adaptation and innovation. On this shoot, passion had to be matched by patience.

One of the most significant inventions – certainly the one Cameron appreciated most – was the 'Simulcam' system, which for the first time in VFX history enabled a filmmaker to see, on their camera monitor, performance-captured digital characters interacting with live-action characters and sets, and thereby better direct and unify the scene, right there and then, rather than piecing it all together months later in post-production.

This development proved invaluable when filming the sequence that Cameron said was the most complex he had ever shot, when Jake and Neytiri (riding a thanator) battle an AMP Suit-wearing Quaritch in a furious climactic showdown that is the inverse of *Aliens*' final fight. (As is the whole film, with the 'aliens' – actually the indigenous population – having our sympathy and the humans being the villainous outsiders.) This sequence required five different characters – one human, two Na'vi, one robot and one monster – on four different scales, while combining CGI with live action. Cameron estimated it took 15 months to figure out. 'It's been a nightmare,' he said.

Even more important than perfecting the action, the director insisted, was ensuring that the full emotional range of the actors' performances shone through the digital characters. This was not just motion capture, he liked to say; this was

**ABOVE:** Sigourney Weaver reunited with Cameron to play Dr Grace Augustine, here seen in her avatar form.

'emotion capture'. To help him achieve it, he smartly partnered up with New Zealand's Weta Digital, the same VFX company that had so impressively created Gollum, and then the eponymous giant ape (also played by Andy Serkis) in Peter Jackson's 2005 *King Kong* remake. And, sure enough, under the supervision of Joe Letteri, Weta delivered. That Saldaña's performance as Neytiri was not included among *Avatar*'s nine Oscar nominations said less about the quality of her work than it did about the acting community's misunderstanding of the performance-capture process, seen as animation rather than a more advanced form of prosthetic make-up.

Of course, one of the Oscars Avatar *did* win was for visual effects, and deservedly so. Pandora presented a full-on photoreal-yet-phantasmagorical ecosystem, the result of extensive research and scientific consultation as well as painstaking performance and animation. The 3D was also far superior to anything seen in cinemas before, so finely calibrated it did not cause headaches and image-ghosting like it had during its last fad in the 1980s. '*Avatar* is a gob-smacking sensory wow, setting an immediate new benchmark for the blockbuster,' wrote Tim Robey in *The Telegraph* on the film's December 2009 release. 'Anyone with half an interest in what the future of film might look like is going to want to see it.'

And many people did. Incredibly, it took *Avatar* only 39 days to break the box-office record set by Cameron himself 12 years earlier with *Titanic*. By the end of its theatrical run, it had taken just over $2.9 billion, making it the highest-grossing movie ever made. During his 'cliff-dive', Cameron had not knitted a parachute. He had stitched together a glider, which gracefully soared him to new heights. But this did not make him immune to criticism.

By channelling the likes of Kipling and Haggard, and embracing the archetypal narrative of 'the male warrior in an exotic, alien land, overcoming physical challenges and confronting the fears of difference,' he was also arguably infusing his story with retrograde values, not least of which was the white saviour, or white Messiah, fable, more recently characterized by such movies as *Dances With Wolves, Fern Gully: The Last Rainforest* and *The Last Samurai. New York Times* writer David Brooks found the film downright 'offensive' in its application of the fable. 'Natives can either have

**LEFT:** The role of hard-man villain Colonel Miles Quaritch was taken by veteran character actor Stephen Lang.

their history shaped by cruel imperialists or benevolent ones,' he wrote, 'but either way, they are going to be supporting actors in our journey to self-admiration.'

When Cameron was given right of reply by talk show host Charlie Rose, he stated his belief that the white Messiah concept was 'not germane to what the movie's doing'. Historically, he pointed out, indigenous cultures very rarely survived against technologically superior invaders, so it figured that the Na'vi would need Jake's help. Besides, what he was trying to do was use this archetypal situation, couched in the sci-fi genre, to view humanity from the perspective, effectively, of the environment it is currently

destroying. 'We emerge from the end of the film on the side of the Na'vi,' he said. 'We're looking at ourselves now from the outside through a mirror or a lens of this fantasy-allegorical story. So we see ourselves as nature sees us, as the intruder, as the invader, as that which is threatening. And when people have that within the film, they feel a sense of moral outrage.'

There is little doubt of the film's effectiveness in siding its audience against their own species, and the sense of thrill and satisfaction we feel when the Na'vi triumph in the final battle. However, Cameron cannot have his cake and eat it. Jake Sully *is* literally a white Messiah, proclaimed by the Na'vi as a legendary 'Toruk Makto' after he somewhat easily tames the apex predator of Pandora's skies to rouse them into battle against his own kind. Though in the film's final scene, he does entirely shed his physical humanity, beginning a second life in his vat-grown Na'vi form.

And what of the claims that *Avatar* would bring about a second life for cinema, with its game-changing VFX techniques and deployment of 3D intended, to some degree, to lure eyeballs away from smartphone screens and streaming services? Certainly, the methods developed by Cameron and his teams

found widespread application in Hollywood, and facilitated a huge progression in VFX-based filmmaking, resulting in a rejuvenated *Planet of the Apes* series (starring none other than Andy Serkis) and further pushing the horizons of superhero cinema. But, though it proliferated like never before, 3D never took hold as the theatrical norm, and felt more like a ticket-price-inflating bolt-on than a true experiential revolution. Meanwhile, director Christopher Nolan would highlight the comparable spectacle of *downplaying* CGI and shooting on IMAX in blockbusters such as *Inception* and *Interstellar*. And despite *Avatar*'s huge success, its fandom

**ABOVE:** For all its heavy messaging and problematic tropes, *Avatar* doubtlessly delivers on action spectacle.

maintained at the cult level, bubbling away at the fringes rather than impacting the mainstream like that of *Star Wars* or Marvel. 'There's scepticism in the marketplace around, "Oh, did it ever make any real cultural impact?",' admitted Cameron in 2022. '"Can anybody even remember the characters' names?"'

This latter factor was down to the curious fact that *Avatar* was not a franchise in the corporate sense, bombarding the culture on multiple platforms as the years went by. Sure, there were action figures, books and video games, but Cameron remained the dominant individual creative force, and when it came to cinematic adventures on Pandora, he was not delegating. Nor was he rushing to build an empire. Quite the opposite, it seemed. Twelve years passed between *Titanic* and *Avatar*. But *Avatar*'s sequel – Cameron's next film as director – would take even longer to arrive.

*'Family is a fortress'*

# AVATAR: THE WAY OF WATER
## 2022

James Cameron's sequel to *Avatar* was originally slated for December 2014. It was intended as the first of two he would make for 20th Century Fox in a September 2010 deal (which, uniquely, also committed the studio to co-funding his Avatar Alliance Foundation, a non-profit organization that focuses on the environment and Indigenous rights). Publicly, it was a predictable commitment to continuing this new cinematic world he had created. Privately, he was not so sure. The studio, he later said, had

**ABOVE:** Lo'ak (Britain Dalton) befriends the whale-like Payakan, who has been wounded by human intruders.

simply 'amused themselves' by announcing the release date, while the sheer success of the original raised the bar for its follow-up beyond viable reach, he felt. 'When you've done something that's been that transcendent in terms of success, do you really want to try and do that again?'

Just as he had in the wake of *Titanic*'s triumph, Cameron instead slipped away from the clamour of Hollywood for the intense quiet of the deep, and on 26 March 2012 set a very different record by becoming the first person to solo dive to the deepest part of the world's oceans in the Mariana Trench, reaching just over 3,600 metres below sea level in a self-designed submarine (documented in the 2014 National Geographic film *Deepsea Challenge 3D*). Meanwhile, as the creation of the Avatar Alliance Foundation suggested, he was living *Avatar*'s environmental themes, advocating for Indigenous groups in Brazil, and investing in a Canadian pea-protein factory to help promote a climate-friendly vegan diet.

He also, finally, settled into family life with Suzy Amis, raising three children with her, plus one older offspring each from their previous marriages. Though it was hardly plain sailing. At one point, Cameron reported, his kids sat him down and heavily critiqued his parenting. He was away half the time, they complained, and when he was around he tried to compensate for his absence by barking orders and being overly strict. Cameron apparently took this on board; 'I'm much more easy-going now,' he insisted in 2022.

It was Cameron's own arc as a parent that finally inspired him to return to Pandora. In 2013, he put together a new *Avatar* treatment, which he described as 'the story of the family that [Jake Sully] creates on Pandora'. Artistically speaking, he said, 'I'm writing what I know'. So rather than immediately picking up with Jake and Neytiri, the sequel would give them a decade-and-a-half together as parents before launching into their next humanity-provoked challenge. He gave the Sullys five children – the same number as he and Amis – to whom Jake has become 'the asshole dad', balancing his sense of world-saving responsibility as a guerilla-war leader with his need to be present as a father. 'The overarching idea is, the family is our fortress,' Cameron said while publicizing the film. 'It's our greatest weakness and our greatest strength. I thought, "I can write the hell out of this."'

He certainly did. Cameron's treatment was no fewer than 1,300 pages long. It covered far more than a single sequel. This, he realized, was *four* films' worth of material: a full-on 'swing for the fences' saga that he likened to Peter Jackson's *The Lord of the Rings*. Except, unlike Jackson, he did not have JRR Tolkien's books and extensive lore to draw upon. 'So I need to go be Tolkien, and *then* I can go be Peter Jackson,' Cameron said. 'A little bit cheeky and ambitious.' After cutting the treatment to 800 pages, he handed it over to a team of writers, many with TV experience, whom he had hired to pin it all down into separate chapters, with *Rise of the Planet of the Apes* screenwriting couple Rick Jaffa and Amanda Silver ultimately sharing the script credit with Cameron on the first sequel, *The Way of Water*.

**ABOVE:** Jake (Sam Worthington) bonds with a different kind of flying beast in this movie: the skimwing.

Despite the saga's huge scope, he decided to keep the action bound to Pandora and its different Na'vi cultures, rather than considering other worlds and aliens. Unlike most movie planets, which tend to feature a single biome (such as the endless deserts of Tatooine in *Star Wars* and Arrakis in *Dune*), Cameron determined that Pandora should be at least as ecologically diverse as his own world. 'Earth has the Arctic, the Antarctic, the rainforest, the desert and the mountains,' he said. 'All different biomes. And in doing my research on Indigenous culture, you just see an explosion of ideas and wardrobe and belief systems. I thought, "Man, I can spend as many films as I want to make just on Pandora, just by going to different places."'

Unsurprisingly, as the film's title suggests, his first stop was Pandora's ocean. After Jake, Neytiri and their brood are hunted down by Colonel Quaritch (Stephen Lang) – revived in Na'vi-avatar form thanks to a 'sure, whatever' memory-backup download – they decide to quit as warriors and put their family first, retreating from the rainforest of the Omatikaya and joining the mangrove-based Metkayina: a Na'vi people inspired by Polynesian and Melanesian culture, who are physically adapted to life in the sea, with fin-like tails and expanded lung capacity. Cameron was not only drawing on his family for inspiration, but also, once again, his subaquatic excursions, enabling him to dream up his own entire marine zoology, from flying-fish-like skimwings to the huge

tulkuns, which are essentially armoured whales. In a rather on-the-nose spin on the original film's environmental message, these intelligent but non-aggressive creatures are hunted by humanity just as whales are on Earth, thanks to their production of a precious elixir that prevents aging in humans. This yields a crowd-pleasing nature-fightback moment when a young outcast tulkun named Payakan, who befriends the Sullys' youngest son Lo'ak (Britain Dalton), decides to aid the Na'vi and take revenge on his nautical hunters. All of which meant that, for the third time in his career, Cameron was committing to the extended tribulation of a heavily water-based shoot. Except this time, he was doing it with performance capture – something that had never been attempted before.

Early in the film's R&D phase, Cameron's performance-capture team tried to convince him to shoot dry-for-wet, with actors suspended on wires. But this looked 'funny' he said, and lacked 'the real water physics' he needed. This was less about spectacle than giving the film a baseline of acceptable reality. Dry-for-wet could never, for instance, replicate the realness of a swimmer being splashed in the face, and the effect that has on the way they

**ABOVE:** *Titanic*'s Kate Winslet returns to Planet Cameron as Metkayina leader Ronal (left), alongside Cliff Curtis as her husband Tonowari.

deliver their dialogue. 'There's a huge benefit right out of the gate by doing it legitimately in the water,' said VFX supervisor Richard Baneham, 'which is the credibility of the performance.'

Aside from waterproofing all the equipment, the main problem with shooting motion capture underwater was that the Volume cameras' infrared beams would refract. And while switching to ultraviolet solved this, there was the additional issue that the rippling surface would create interference in the signals sent to the computers. Cameron suggested a variation on his light-blocking black–bead technique for *The Abyss*, which was to have a layer of hollow white polymer balls on the surface of their water Volume that gently diffused the light.

This Volume was constructed at Manhattan Beach Studios in California, in a purpose-built 250,000-gallon tank that, at

**ABOVE:** Sigourney Weaver plays 14-year-old Na'vi Kiri, while also making a cameo in human form as Kiri's mother Grace.

36 metres long, 18 metres wide and 9 metres deep, was big enough to recreate oceanic conditions, provided by such hardware as a pair of 2-metre-diameter ship propellers (to generate currents of up to 10 knots) and a moving, tilting platform (to replicate shore conditions for certain scenes). Cameron described it as his 'complete Swiss army system'. Though further innovation was still required: whenever characters were half in and half out of the water, a second, air Volume needed to be placed directly above the water Volume. Each Volume's set of motion-capture data had to be separately pushed to a tertiary server, which, in around an eighth of a second, combined them back together and presented the floating character as a single, whole figure on Cameron's virtual camera screen.

Similar to the experience of making *Avatar*, production on *The Way of Water* (which began shooting in 2017, five years before its release) became a matter of highly technical problem-solving on the fly. 'That's the way he's always done it,' said cinematographer Russell Carpenter, who had previously worked with Cameron on *True Lies* and *Titanic*. 'He's always said, "I don't know how to make this film, but we're gonna know when we've made the film." That's a daring I just don't see in many people.'

Sometimes a solution needed to be very simple rather than highly technical. Such as the problem of the air bubbles. It soon became apparent that, if the underwater actors and crew used scuba gear, the bubbles it unavoidably emitted would jumble up the images, due to the way they refracted light between a performer's marker dots and the Volume cameras. So, Cameron decided that nobody should have any breathing equipment at all, and brought in freediving guru Kirk Krack to teach both actors and crew how to hold their breath for long periods underwater. 'It's the hardest thing I've ever had to do,' said Sam Worthington, who returned as Jake. 'You're dealing with the restrictions of freediving, the constraints of motion capture underwater, and you're trying to keep an emotional journey while you're innately struggling with the fear of dying.'

One of Worthington's co-stars was a Cameron water-shoot veteran. Despite having gone on the record back in 1997 about her reluctance to work with him again, *Titanic*'s Kate Winslet plunged back in as Metkayina matriarch Ronal (who, in a Cameron fierce-female first, goes into battle while heavily pregnant). 'I just loved it so much, my gosh,' she said of the freediving, during which she achieved an astonishing breath-hold of seven minutes and 14 seconds. She was also very happy to be working with Cameron again, whom she confirmed was 'a more chilled-out guy these days. He's definitely mellowed.'

Another returning actor was Sigourney Weaver, this time taking the role of Grace Augustine's 14-year-old daughter Kiri – a Na'vi born from Grace's inert avatar, which, we learn in another 'sure, whatever' moment, became mysteriously pregnant. Even aside from the freediving, playing someone 54 years younger provided Weaver with a whole new acting challenge. 'I had to work in a completely different way than I've ever worked,' she said. 'That was very exciting for me.' Though Cameron apparently thought she would find it a breeze. 'He was very funny. He said, "You're so immature, this will be easy for you"!

The other Sully children were played by newcomer actors their own age – though they all grew up by five years between the start of shooting and the film's release, which proved particularly challenging in the case of Jack Champion as Spider. Being a human wild-child Sully adoptee (revealed as the offspring of bad-guy Quaritch, no less), his aging could not be disguised by Na'vi appearance, which meant that in addition to shooting *The Way of Water* between 2017 and 2020, Cameron also had to shoot the third *Avatar* film *Fire And Ash*, as well as the first act of the untitled fourth *Avatar* (up to a point in the story where, the director has revealed, a big time jump happens).

**BELOW:** Jack Champion as the Sullys' adopted human son – also the biological child of the resurrected Colonel Quaritch.

## The fate of the Terminator: *Terminator: Dark Fate* (2019)

While working on *The Way of Water*, Cameron returned to the film series he had seemingly abandoned years earlier, after point-blank refusing to direct 2003's *Terminator 3: Rise of the Machines* (a job that went to Jonathan Mostow), despite Arnold Schwarzenegger's continued involvement. McG's future-war-set *Terminator Salvation* followed in 2009 (without Schwarzenegger), with Alan Taylor's *Terminator Genisys* attempting a reboot in 2015 via a new timeline, Schwarzenegger's return as an aged T-800, and a recast Sarah Connor (Emilia Clarke).

After *Genisys* flopped, the rights owners Skydance Productions pivoted, with *Deadpool 2* director Tim Miller, to a concept that would ignore the three non-Cameron sequels and pick up directly after *Judgment Day*. As such, Miller wanted Cameron involved. So, excited by the idea of doing 'a legit sequel to *Terminator 2*,' he came on board the sixth *Terminator* movie, *Dark Fate,* as a producer, with a 'story by' credit.

The film brings back Linda Hamilton as Sarah and Schwarzenegger as a T-800, which has integrated with humanity over the years, after fulfilling its mission to kill John Connor in 1998. It is an interesting twist, though the film gets less interesting as Sarah and 'Carl' (as the T-800 names itself) become involved in yet another killer-from-the-future chase. New AI threat 'Legion' sends a liquid metal/endoskeleton hybrid 'Rev-9' (Gabriel Luna) back in time to kill the next anti-machine resistance leader Dani Ramos (Natalia Reyes), with a cybernetically enhanced future-human named Grace (Mackenzie Davis) dispatched to protect her.

The film bombed at the box office, making a $122.6 million loss, and sequel plans were nixed. 'There was nothing in the movie for a new audience,' reflected Cameron in 2024, noting that a 63-year-old Hamilton and a 72-year-old Schwarzenegger did not appeal to their core 15–25-year-old audience. 'This is not your father's *Terminator*. This is your grandfather's *Terminator*. People just didn't show up.'

Even so, Cameron still has plans to revive his chrome-skulled baby, to explore the themes of AI threat and everyday people empowering themselves to fight it. 'There are certain things that are of the fabric of *Terminator* that have nothing to do with the Linda Hamilton of it all, or the Arnold of it,' he said. 'So I have no doubt that subsequent *Terminator* films will not only be possible, but they'll kick ass.'

Spider's presence also vastly increased the number of scenes shared by 2.7-metre-tall Na'vi and regular-sized humans, creating yet another challenge for the production. 'We would oftentimes have two sets: one at the Na'vi scale, one at the human scale,' said producer Jon Landau. 'And we had to tie those two things together, and they had to be in lockstep so everything matched.'

In the end, *The Way of Water* cost $350 million and contained a whopping 3,350 visual effects shots, once again impeccably rendered by Weta Digital in New Zealand – now Cameron's home – to a level of quality that the director boasted was unmatched by any other effects house in the world. And, despite 3D not really taking hold after *Avatar*'s release, he once again committed to the format, even shooting some of the underwater and action scenes at a higher frame rate of 48 frames per second, to crystallise the immersive realism of his entirely computer-fabricated world.

As with the first film, there was a real sense on release of witnessing a bold new benchmark in digital effects, both through the presentation of emotional performance – from the Sullys' wonder at the undersea world to their furious grief at the death of eldest child Neteyam (Jamie Flatters) – and through the creation of a seemingly palpable environment, in this case a vast, sparkling ocean teeming with invented creatures. '*Avatar: The Way of Water* has scenes that will make your eyes pop, your head spin and your soul race,' wrote critic Owen Gleiberman in *Variety*. '[It] is braided with sequences that exist almost solely for their sculptured imagistic magic. It's truly a movie crossed with a virtual-reality theme-park ride.'

However, the film's storytelling and dialogue were widely criticized for lacking the substance of its visuals. 'The story, which might fill a 30-minute cartoon, is stretched as if by some AI program into a three-hour movie of epic tweeness,' wrote

Peter Bradshaw in *The Guardian*. 'The floatingly bland plot is like a children's story without the humour; a YA story without the emotional wound; an action thriller without the hard edge of real excitement.'

Cameron's shift in perspective towards the Sully offspring certainly dilutes one of the original film's strongest elements: Zoë Saldaña's Neytiri, here sidelined into a fussing mother role, at least until the climactic conflict. But it feels undeserving of such a scathing response. Once again, Cameron uses archetypes and familiar tropes to balance his exotic setting, and thereby broaden its emotional accessibility. And once again he succeeded in connecting with his audience on a global scale; the movie grossed over $2.3 billion on release, making it the third biggest in cinema history.

As for the criticisms of his dialogue, Cameron had a characteristically punchy response. 'I have a lower cringe factor than, apparently, a lot of people do around the dialogue that I write,' he said in 2024. 'But fuck them. You know what? Let me see your three-out-of-the-four highest-grossing films – then we'll talk about dialogue effectiveness.'

*The Way of Water*'s detractors need to brace themselves, because Cameron's immediate filmmaking future remains tall, blue and feline. The next instalment in the *Avatar* franchise, *Fire and Ash*, introduces the Na'vi 'Ash People' alongside a host of new creatures, such as the medusoid – a giant flying jellyfish – and the stingray-like windray, at last brought to life from Cameron's *Xenogenesis* concept artwork. However, he is well aware that transporting audiences to new biomes and delivering high-def spectacle is not enough to sustain his saga. *Fire and Ash*, he said early in 2025, will 'get people to care more about the characters than about the shock of the new. It's a different kind of engagement with the audience.' The abiding theme is how we deal with grief, something that had been on his mind over the past few years, what with the unexpected deaths of his friends and collaborators Bill Paxton, James Horner and Jon Landau.

There are other, non-Pandoran projects in development, too, Cameron has revealed. The most intriguing marks a return to one of his favourite subjects: nuclear devastation. In September 2024, it was revealed that he'd purchased the rights to the books *To Hell and Back: The Last Train From Hiroshima* and *Ghosts of Hiroshima*,

**BELOW:** Neytiri (Zoë Saldaña) and Jake suffer a tragic loss during the film's final confrontation.

written by Charles Pellegrino. Relating the true story of Tsutomu Yamaguchi, who survived the bombings of both Hiroshima and Nagasaki in August 1945, Cameron's adaptation will tell a story he's been 'wrestling with' for years. But it will have to wait until his *Avatar* schedule allows, and he apparently remains committed to further instalments in that series.

And why wouldn't he? The *Avatar* movies, Cameron has stated, provide him with a canvas to say 'everything I need to say about family, about sustainability, about climate, about the natural world – the themes that are important to me.' They hark back to his earliest visions as a high-school kid, imagining worlds that were then far beyond cinema's grasp. They tap into the same innovative creative urges that fuelled him during his formative filmmaking

ABOVE: Concept art from *Avatar*'s third installment *Fire and Ash*, featuring the airborne, jellyfish-like creatures known as medusoids and the windrays that tow them.

years at Roger Corman's studio, and then throughout his career as a purveyor of cutting-edge blockbuster entertainment. They relate closely to his own documented adventures as an explorer of 'inner space'. They embody the values he holds dearest and promotes, both personal and political. They are pure, unfiltered Cameron, seemingly uploaded direct from his imagination, with no expense spared on their execution – the very apotheosis of his career and creative life. As the man himself has pointed out, who other than he could ever pull this off? 'I don't care how smart you are as a director,' he said in 2022, 'you don't know how to do this.'

# Resources

**Introduction**

Keegan, Rebecca, *The Futurist: The Life and Films of James Cameron*, Crown Publishers, 2009

Mooney, Joshua, 'Lasting Impact', *Movieline*, July 1994

Wootton, Adrian, '*Guardian* Interviews at the BFI: James Cameron', *The Guardian*, 13 April 2003

**Chapter One**

Byrge, Duane, 'Camera on Cameron', *The Hollywood Reporter*, 24 November 1986

Cameron, James, *Tech Noir*, Titan Books, 2021

Heard, Christopher, *Dreaming Aloud: The Life and Films of James Cameron*, Doubleday Canada, 1998

Keegan, Rebecca, *The Futurist: The Life and Films of James Cameron*, Crown Publishers, 2009

McDonnell, David and D'Angelo Carr (editors), 'Aliens Direction: James Cameron', *Official Aliens Movie Magazine*, Starlog Group, 1986

Nathan, Ian, *The Terminator Vault*, Aurum Press Limited, 2013

Prince, Chris (editor), *James Cameron's Story of Science Fiction*, Insight Editions, 2018

Rinzler, JW, *The Making of Aliens*, Titan Books, 2020

Shapiro, Marc, *James Cameron: An Unauthorized Biography of the Filmmaker*, Renaissance Books, 2000

'James Cameron', Smartless podcast, 19 December 2022

Turan, Kenneth, 'The *US* Interview', *US*, August 1991

Wootton, Adrian, '*Guardian* Interviews at the BFI: James Cameron', *The Guardian*, 13 April 2003

**Chapter Two**

Byrge, Duane, 'Camera on Cameron', *The Hollywood Reporter*, 24 November 1986

Cameron, James, *Tech Noir*, Titan Books, 2021

Heard, Christopher, *Dreaming Aloud: The Life and Films of James Cameron*, Doubleday Canada, 1998

Keegan, Rebecca, *The Futurist: The Life and Films of James Cameron*, Crown Publishers, 2009

Klein, Andy, 'Three Young Directors', *Los Angeles Reader*, 15 March 1985

Prince, Chris (editor), *James Cameron's Story of Science Fiction*, Insight Editions, 2018

Richardson, John H., 'Iron Jim', *Premiere*, August 1994

Rinzler, JW, *The Making of Aliens*, Titan Books, 2020

Shapiro, Marc, *James Cameron: An Unauthorized Biography of the Filmmaker*, Renaissance Books, 2000

'James Cameron', Smartless podcast, 19 December 2022

Turan, Kenneth, 'The *US* Interview', *US*, August 1991

**Chapter Three**

Bass, George, '*The Terminator* came to me in a dream: a new interview with James Cameron', BFI, 21 April 2021

Chute, David '*The Terminator*: $5 Mil.', *Film Comment*, February 1985

Ellis, Kirk, '*The Terminator*: *THR*'s Review', *The Hollywood Reporter*, 26 October 1984

Heard, Christopher, *Dreaming Aloud: The Life and Films of James Cameron*, Doubleday Canada, 1998

Hewitt, Chris, 'Setting the Future', *Empire*, November 2024

Hurd, Gale Anne, 'Activating Arnold', *Empire*, November 2024

Keegan, Rebecca, *The Futurist: The Life and Films of James Cameron*, Crown Publishers, 2009

Lynskey, Dorian, '*The Terminator*: How James Cameron's "science-fiction slasher film" predicted our fears about AI, 40 years ago', BBC Culture, 18 October 2024

Nathan, Ian, *The Terminator Vault*, Aurum Press Limited, 2013

Shapiro, Marc, *James Cameron: An Unauthorized Biography of the Filmmaker*, Renaissance Books, 2000

'James Cameron', Smartless podcast, 19 December 2022

*The Making of The Terminator: A Retrospective*, The Terminator UK Blu-ray


**Chapter Four**

*Superior Firepower: The Making of Aliens*, The Alien Quadrilogy DVD

Goodman, Walter, 'Film: Sigourney Weaver in *Aliens*', *The New York Times*, 18 July 1986

Heard, Christopher, *Dreaming Aloud: The Life and Films of James Cameron*, Doubleday Canada, 1998

'James Cameron', *The Hour with George Stroumboulopoulos*, CBC, 8 October 2008

Keegan, Rebecca, *The Futurist: The Life and Films of James Cameron*, Crown Publishers, 2009

McDonnell, David and D'Angelo Carr (editors), 'Aliens Direction: James Cameron', *Aliens: The Official Movie Magazine*, Starlog Group, 1986

McDonnell, David and D'Angelo Carr (editors), 'Sigourney Weaver: Codename Ripley', *Aliens: The Official Movie Magazine*, Starlog Group, 1986

McDonnell, David and D'Angelo Carr (editors), 'Alien Biology: Stan Winston', *Aliens: The Official Movie Magazine*, Starlog Group, 1986

Nathan, Ian, 'Welcome to my Bug Hunt', *Empire*, Summer 2024

Ressner, Jeffrey, 'In Search of the Miraculous', *DGA Quarterly*, Summer 2008

Rinzler, JW, *The Making of Aliens*, Titan Books, 2020

Shapiro, Marc, *James Cameron: An Unauthorized Biography of the Filmmaker*, Renaissance Books, 2000

*Variety* Staff, 'Aliens', *Variety*, 31 December 1985

*Variety* Staff, 'The best movie sequels of all time', *Variety*, 2 March 2023


**Chapter Five**

'Under Pressure: Making *The Abyss*', *The Abyss Special Edition* UK DVD

Ansen, David, 'Under Fire, Underwater', *Newsweek*, 14 August 1989

Byrge, Duane, 'Camera on Cameron', *The Hollywood Reporter*, 24 November 1986

Harmetz, Aljean, '*The Abyss*: A Foray Into Deep Waters', *The New York Times*, 6 August 1989

Heard, Christopher, *Dreaming Aloud: The Life and Films of James Cameron*, Doubleday Canada, 1998

Kasindorf, Martin, 'Fox Plunges Into *The Abyss*: Far behind schedule and millions over budget, the film arrives – but is it too late to cash in?', *Los Angeles Times*, 6 August 1989

Keegan, Rebecca, *The Futurist: The Life and Films of James Cameron*, Crown Publishers, 2009

Kempley, Rita, 'Saturated Sci-fi', *The Washington Post*, 9 August 1989

Newman, Kim, '*The Abyss*', *Empire*, November 1989

Shapiro, Marc, *James Cameron: An Unauthorized Biography of the Filmmaker*, Renaissance Books, 2000

Turan, Kenneth, 'The *US* interview: James Cameron', *US*, August 1991

## Chapter Six

Byrge, Duane, '*Terminator 2: Judgment Day*', *The Hollywood Reporter*, 3 July 1991

Chase, Donald, 'On the set of *Terminator 2*', *Entertainment Weekly*, 12 July 1991

Cooney, Jenny, 'Harder Than The Rest', *Empire*, September 1991

Field, Syd, 'James Cameron *Terminator 2: Judgment Day* (Part 1)', Syd Field: The Art of Visual Storytelling Blog [undated]

Heard, Christopher, *Dreaming Aloud: The Life and Films of James Cameron*, Doubleday Canada, 1998

Hewitt, Chris, 'Setting the Future', *Empire*, November 2024

Keegan, Rebecca, *The Futurist: The Life and Films of James Cameron*, Crown Publishers, 2009

Nathan, Ian, *The Terminator Vault*, Aurum Press Limited, 2013

Shay, Don and Duncan, Jody, *T2: The Making of Terminator 2: Judgment Day*, Titan Books, 1991

Siegel, Alan, 'The Tin Man Gets His Heart: An Oral History of *Terminator 2: Judgment Day*', The Ringer, 30 June 2021

*The Making of Terminator 2: Judgment Day*, *Terminator 2: Judgment Day: Ultimate Edition* US DVD

Turan, Kenneth, 'Review: He said he'd be back... Arnold and *Terminator 2* return with a vengeance', *Los Angeles Times*, 3 July 1991

## Chapter Seven

Ebert, Roger, '*True Lies*', *Chicago Sun-Times*, 15 July 1994

Hajari, Nisid and Broeske Pat H, 'Racism and sexism in *True Lies*?', *Entertainment Weekly*, 5 August 1994

Heard, Christopher, *Dreaming Aloud: The Life and Films of James Cameron*, Doubleday Canada, 1998

Hobson, Louis B, 'Sequel talk true or lies?' Jam! Showbiz, 4 March 2003

Keegan, Rebecca, *The Futurist: The Life and Films of James Cameron*, Crown Publishers, 2009

Richardson, John H, 'Iron Jim', *Premiere*, August 1994

Shapiro, Marc, *James Cameron: An Unauthorized Biography of the Filmmaker*, Renaissance Books, 2000

Thompson, Anne, '5 True Lies about James Cameron', *Entertainment Weekly*, 29 July 1994

*Fear Is Not An Option: The Making of True Lies*, *True Lies* UK Blu-ray

## Chapter Eight

Byrge, Duane, '*Titanic*', *The Hollywood Reporter*, 3 November 1997

Cameron, James, *Tech Noir*, Titan Books, 2021

Cameron, James, '*Titanic* Is a Tough Shoot; What Else Is New?', *Los Angeles Times*, 5 May 1997

Gritten, David, 'Back From the Abyss', *Los Angeles Times*, 11 May 1997

Heard, Christopher, *Dreaming Aloud: The Life and Films of James Cameron*, Doubleday Canada, 1998

'James Cameron', *The Hour with George Stroumboulopoulos*, CBC, 8 October 2008

Keegan, Rebecca, *The Futurist: The Life and Films of James Cameron*, Crown Publishers, 2009

Lane, Anthony, *Nobody's Perfect*, Picador, 2002

Maslin, Janet, 'A Spectacle as Sweeping as the Sea', *The New York Times*, 19 December 1997

Puig, Claudia, 'Epic-Size Troubles on *Titanic*', *Los Angeles Times*, 19 April 1997

NPR staff, 'James Cameron: Diving Deep, dredging Up *Titanic*', *Morning Edition*, NPR, 30 March 2012

Parisi, Paula, *Titanic and the Making of James Cameron: The Inside Story of the Three-Year Adventure That Rewrote Motion Picture History*, Newmarket Press, 1998

Ressner, Jeffrey, 'In Search of the Miraculous', *DGA Quarterly Magazine*, Summer 2008

Rich, Katey, 'What You're Still Getting Wrong About *Titanic*, According to James Cameron', *Vanity Fair*, 5 December 2023

Rose, Charlie, 'James Cameron', 18 December 1997

Smith, Steven, 'Ship's Star Trouper', *Los Angeles Times*, 14 December 1997

**Chapter Nine**

Keegan, Rebecca, *The Futurist: The Life and Films of James Cameron*, Crown Publishers, 2009

Parisi, Paula, *Titanic and the Making of James Cameron: The Inside Story of the Three-Year Adventure That Rewrote Motion Picture History*, Newmarket Press, 1998

Rampton, James, 'James Cameron: My *Titanic* obsession', *The Independent*, 9 August 2005

Richardson, John H, 'Iron Jim', *Premiere*, August 1994

Rose, Charlie, 'James Cameron', 7 August 2014

'James Cameron', Smartless podcast, 19 December 2022

Wootton, Adrian, '*Guardian* interviews at the BFI: James Cameron', *The Guardian*, 13 April 2003

**Chapter Ten**

Brooks, David, 'The Messiah Complex,' *The New York Times*, 7 January 2010

Duncan, Jody and Fitzpatrick, Lisa, *The Making of Avatar*, Abrams, 2010

Dyer, James, 'The New World', *Empire*, October 2009

Jensen, Jeff, 'James Cameron talks *Avatar*', *Entertainment Weekly*, 15 January 2007

Keegan, Rebecca, 'Inside James Cameron's Billion-Dollar Bet on *Avatar*', *The Hollywood Reporter*, 30 November 2022

McNary, Dave, 'James Cameron Producing *Alita: Battle Angel*' with Robert Rodriguez Directing, *Variety*, 14 October 2015

Robey, Tim, '*Avatar*: changing the face of film forever', *The Telegraph*, 19 December 2009

Rose, Charlie, 'James Cameron', 17 December 2009

Rose, Charlie, 'James Cameron', 17 February 2010

**Chapter Eleven**

'James Cameron compares upcoming *Avatar* sequels to *The Godfather* from his walnut farm in New Zealand', The Associated Press, 16 December 2013

*Inside Pandora's Box*, *Avatar: The Way of Water* UK Blu-Ray

*Avatar: The Way of Water* production notes, Disney

Bradshaw, Peter, '*Avatar: The Way of Water*', *The Guardian*, 15 December 2022

De Semlyen, Nick, 'Ready to go back?', *Empire*, February 2025

Dockterman, Eliana, 'James Cameron Is Reconsidering a Few Things', *TIME*, 16 February 2023

Fleming Jr, Mike, 'James Cameron Buys *Ghosts of Hiroshima* Book and Commits to Film as his Next Project as *Avatar* Production Permits', *Deadline*, 16 September 2024

Freer, Ian, 'Going Deeper', *Empire,* August 2022

Freer, Ian, '*Avatar: The Way of Water*: Sigourney Weaver on Playing Na'vi Teenager Kiri And Reuniting With James Cameron', *Empire* online, 29 November 2022

Gleiberman, Owen, '*Avatar: The Way of Water*', *Variety*, 13 December 2022

Hewitt, Chris, 'Setting the Future', *Empire*, November 2024

Jolin, Dan, '*Avatar: The Way of Water* cinematographer talks challenges of filming 3D underwater, relationship with James Cameron', *Screen Daily*, 15 January 2023

Jolin, Dan, interview with Richard Baneham, conducted for *Screen International* on 14 February 2023

Keegan, Rebecca, 'Inside Cameron's Billion-Dollar Bet on *Avatar*', *The Hollywood Reporter*, 30 November 2022

Lang, Brent, '"Minds Will Be Blown": James Cameron tells Robert Rodriguez Why *Avatar 2* Is "Dangerous" and the Key Advice Guillermo Del Toro Gave Him', *Variety*, 14 December 2022

Rose, Steve, 'It's got to be an experience, first and foremost: James Cameron, Sigourney Weaver and Kate Winslet on the return of *Avatar*', *The Guardian*, 16 December 2022

# Index

# Bibliography

Cameron, James, *Tech Noir*, Titan Books, 2021

Duncan, Jody and Fitzpatrick, Lisa, *The Making of Avatar*, Abrams, 2010

French, Sean, *BFI Modern Classics: The Terminator*, BFI Publishing, 1996

Heard, Christopher, *Dreaming Aloud: The Life and Films of James Cameron*, Doubleday Canada, 1998

Keegan, Rebecca, *The Futurist: The Life and Films of James Cameron*, Crown Publishers, 2009

Lane, Anthony, *Nobody's Perfect*, Picador, 2002

Nathan, Ian, *The Terminator Vault*, Aurum Press Limited, 2013

Parisi, Paula, *Titanic and the Making of James Cameron: The Inside Story of the Three-Year Adventure That Rewrote Motion Picture History*, Newmarket Press, 1998

Prince, Chris (editor), *James Cameron's Story of Science Fiction*, Insight Editions, 2018

Rinzler, JW, *The Making of Aliens*, Titan Books, 2020

Shapiro, Marc, *James Cameron: An Unauthorized Biography of the Filmmaker*, Renaissance Books, 2000

Shay, Don and Duncan, Jody, *T2: The Making of Terminator 2: Judgment Day*, Titan Books, 1991

# Picture credits

**Alamy Stock Photo:** 4/5: ©TRISTAR PICTURES/courtesy Maximum Film; 6, 22/23, 178, 180/181, 186/187, 194/195: ©20th Century Fox/courtesy Landmark Media; 8/9, 75, 135, 196/197: ©20th Century Fox/courtesy Cinematic Collection; 10/11, 80/81, 92, 113, 114/115, 127, 130, 141, 153, 169, 184: Moviestore Collection Ltd; 13, 192: RGR Collection; 14, 90/91, 98, 140: ©20th Century Fox/courtesy Everett Collection; 17: LES BREAULT; 18/19: ©MGM/courtesy Allstar Picture Library Ltd; 21: ©Buena Vista Pictures/courtesy Entertainment Pictures; 24/25, 42, 46/47, 52, 58/59, 63/63: ©Orion Pictures/courtesy Landmark Media; 26, 35, 160/161: United Archives GmbH/IFA Film; 28/29, 87: Photo 12; 30: Photo12/Paul Sterling Hodara/New World Pictures; 31: Everett Collection Inc; 32/33: ©New World Releasing/Courtesy Everett Collection; 37: ©Columbia/courtesy Cinematic Collection; 38: ©Columbia/courtesy AJ Pics; 40/41, 85, 102, 104/105, 124/125, 132/133, 137, 165, 204/205, 214/215: Pictorial Press Ltd; 45: ©Orion Pictures/courtesy Album; 48, 55, 57: ©Orion Pictures/courtesy Cinematic Collection; 51: ©Orion Pictures/courtesy AJ Pics; 64, 70, 146, 150/151, 157: ©20th Century Fox/courtesy Maximum Film; 67, 68, 72, 76, 138, 143, 144, 183: ©20th Century Fox/courtesy AJ Pics; 82, 176: ©20th Century Fox/courtesy Album; 95: United Archives GmbH/Impress; 97: Photo12/7e Art/20th Century Fox; 99: United Archives GmbH/TBM; 101, 122: United Archives GmbH/kpa Publicity Stills; 108: ©TRISTAR PICTURES/courtesy AJ Pics; 111: ©TRISTAR PICTURES/courtesy Everett Collection Inc; 118: Photo 12/Archives du 7e Art; 120/121: © 1991 Carolco/courtesy PictureLux/The Hollywood Archive; 131: ©20th CENTURY FOX/RGR Collection; 158/159: ©20th Century Fox/Allstar Picture Library/SPORTSPHOTO; 162: ©Buena Vista Pictures/courtesy Cinematic Collection; 168, 171t: ©Walt Disney Pictures/courtesy AJ Pics; 171b, 172: ©Walt Disney Pictures/courtesy Maximum Film; 173: ©Buena Vista Pictures/Courtesy Everett Collection; 175: ©Buena Vista Pictures/courtesy Maximum Film; 191, 206/207: ©20th Century Fox/courtesy Entertainment Pictures; 198, 200/201, 203: Photo12/7e Art/20th Century Studios; 209: BFA/20th Century Studios; 213: ©20th Century Studios/courtesy PictureLux/The Hollywood Archive/THA.

# Acknowledgements

Thanks, as ever, to my ace editorial team: Kerry Enzor and Andrew Roff at Quercus; Julia Shone at Greenfinch; and Anna Southgate (who makes the kindest cuts). Plus designer Ginny Zeal, for making my words look so great, and Luke Bird, for his super-cool cover art.

I'm also once more hugely grateful to my better half Lucy Jolin for being my first reader, and putting up with my long absences in the company of killer robots and aliens. I'd also like to thank Dorian Lynskey and Nick de Semlyen for their ongoing support and advice, as well as providing some specific pointers for the *Terminator* and *Avatar* sequel chapters, respectively. Not to forget my *Senet* magazine co-founder James Hunter for his patience while I was deep in the Cameron-sphere, and all the commissioning editors I had to neglect while writing this book. Primarily: James Dyer, Alex Godfrey, Chris Hewitt, John Nugent and Beth Webb of *Empire* magazine; Charles Gant and Matt Mueller of *Screen International*; and Phil de Semlyen of *Time Out* London.